Praise for *Findi*

I know Jeff to be wholly committed to C....ist and the flourishing of his church, and the humble, candid, and thought-provoking journey he's told through *Finding Our Way* is further evidence of that. Jeff's leadership, and the journey I walked with my Southridge family for the better part of two decades, played a critical role in my understanding of the mission of God and his church, and what it means to live a lifestyle of full devotion to Jesus. Our church's "Action" focus, and model of extending compassion and justice both locally and globally, had a particularly profound impact on my life and leadership. (Not the least of which included introducing me to the organization I now lead.) I'm confident the insights Jeff provides in these pages will challenge and influence many leaders to advance God's revealed vision for his church at home and around the world, as it did for me.

—ALLISON ALLEY
Compassion Canada

Reading this book feels like a special invitation to sit at the leadership table of some tremendous church leaders as they fight with resilience and grace to make their local church a brighter and more loving light in the world. Jeff Lockyer allows us to peel back the curtain and learn from the victories and mistakes of his team. I believe *Finding Our Way* will prove to be immensely helpful to all those who care deeply about the future of the church. I have had the opportunity to visit Southridge and dialogue with several of their leaders. Watching them continue to ask probing questions with humility and truth-telling gives me great hope for the church of tomorrow. Roll up your sleeves and dig into the practical wisdom found in these pages.

—NANCY BEACH
Leadership Coach, Slingshot Group

Jeff Lockyer has generously opened the curtain so all can see the thoughtful—and painful, and fruitful—journey of a leader who loves Jesus and the Church for which he gave his life. With refreshing candour, Jeff shares the lessons, including some of the mistakes, he and his fellow teammates at Southridge have lived through as they continually stretched themselves to engage with God. Wonderfully, he doesn't try to present an archetype of the ideal church; his aim is to help all of us be more intentional, more inquisitive, and more dependent on God as we participate with him in the building of his church. Leaders of all descriptions will find this book helpful. Jeff's pragmatic emphasis makes the book highly actionable. His inspired curiosity challenges us to tackle church-building intellectually. And his courageous vulnerability invites us to all engage spiritually. This is perfect . . . because we're all *Finding Our Way*.

—JIM BROWN
President, Strive!
Author, *The Imperfect Board Member*

Our world has changed. The digital revolution combined with a global pandemic has disrupted just about every facet of our lives, including most churches. But Jesus' call to make disciples has not. The problem most leaders are facing is: how do we actually make disciples today with people of all ages and all walks of life? In *Finding Our Way*, Jeff Lockyer takes us into the heart of a thriving church that set up base camp on the frontlines in their city to share Jesus' message and demonstrate his compassion. Jeff dispels the myths and plainly lays out what it looks like for an entire church as they follow the way of Jesus, including the real costs and incredible rewards. *Finding Our Way* is a field guide to get us back on the path of making disciples. For the Christian church, this is our only path into the future.

—TIM DAY
Director, City Movement Canada
Author, *God Enters Stage Left*

Often in my work supporting organizations to create cultures where both men and women can thrive, I find that, when leaders learn what it really takes, they stand down. Jeff Lockyer stood up. He is a leader who reaches across the gap, who is willing to go into tough places, and who crafts real life opportunities for transformative learning. *Finding Our Way* unfolds like a good conversation, moving from hard-won insight, to challenge, encouragement, and back again. In sharing their church's journey Jeff invites us to think more deeply about ours. In this season of unprecedented challenge and opportunity the great gift of this book is its clarion call to build a culture that reflects the heart of God for this generation.

—ELLEN DUFFIELD
Director, BRAVE Women
Author, *The BRAVE Way*

This book is a life's work. Jeff Lockyer shares wisdom nurtured by years of faithful and fruitful ministry. Some of the choices Jeff and his team have made over the years will be immediately applicable, but because he shares their process as well as the learnings, the missteps as well as their conclusions, the book becomes a guide to our own discerning and decisions as church leaders. *Finding Our Way* is less of a road map and more a Fodor's travel guide for all who lead, and for all of us who love Jesus and his church. Highly recommended!

—NEIL & SHAROL JOSEPHSON
Directors, Family Life Canada

I am convicted that the world needs Christ now more than ever! And how will we see the world change for the better, even flourish? Jeff Lockyer's *Finding Our Way* provides a great plan for the church to return to its core purpose of revealing Jesus to the world in the context of the world we live in. For me, this book is worth reading because Jeff has integrity. Yes, I've watched his journey now for over five years and have seen the confidential results of his employee engagement surveys confirm the story he has shared with us. Thanks, Jeff, for shepherding the flock God has entrusted to you and for sharing the Southridge journey.

—AL LOPUS
CEO and Cofounder, Best Christian Workplaces Institute

In *Finding Our Way*, Jeff Lockyer provides a much-needed compass for navigating life in ministry. Lockyer writes from the vantage point of a seasoned, faithful leader. He paints a compelling vision for why full devotion matters and offers tangible guidance in how to structure a church for community transformation. Jeff, thanks for helping us find our way.

—JEFF MANION
Senior Pastor, Ada Bible Church
Author, *The Land Between* and *Dream Big Think Small*

Any congregation that trades its ivy-covered church in wine country for an abandoned school building in a poor urban neighborhood, and then dedicates half of it to the largest hostel for homeless people in the region, is going to catch my attention. Many years ago now, Southridge Community Church did all that, and subsequently won my wholehearted admiration. Jeff Lockyer and his partners in guiding that congregation for over twenty years have done something that gives me hope for the church at large: they've facilitated the conversion of a typically anachronistic, self-serving, and culturally irrelevant "church" into a fulsome, thriving, outward-looking kingdom community.

Most books about church planting or church growth are so full of strategies, actions, worship (entertainment!) idioms and subtle chest-thumping that they read like sales manuals. We do seem to have gotten off track in many ways, and so *Finding Our Way* is a fresh, thought-provoking and humble word. Jeff knows that character matters more than numeric growth; hands-on mission more than razzle-dazzle programs; and the uncertainty that engenders real faith far more than bullet-proof doctrinal statements. While Southridge, as a large, multi-site congregation, has many of the markers of conventional success, if you're looking for a template to accomplish that, this book will be a waste of your time. If, however, you want to be challenged, inspired, and instructed about establishing or re-shaping a church into a real world, in-the-trenches, gospel-living body— then buy it and read it several times!

—GREG PAUL
Sanctuary Toronto
Author, *God in the Alley*, *Resurrecting Religion* and more

Finding Our Way shares experiences and learnings of decades of leadership in a growing, influential, and community-impacting church. The insights presented are certainly of immense value not only for pastors and church leaders but for anyone in a leadership position in any organization. I applaud Jeff for addressing some of the most controversial and important issues of our time and sharing practical ideas on how to lead through them. Although it is not a book that offers advice specifically on how to deal with the effects of the COVID-19 pandemic, the concepts and learnings addressed in it will undoubtedly be of great value to leading during challenging times.

—GARY SCHWAMMLEIN
President Emeritus, Global Leadership Network

Perhaps the most meaningful observation of Jeff Lockyer's insight into church life is that it rings true! Although based on solid theory and research the greatest asset is that it reflects reality. Those who have spent years or decades vitally involved in a local church will see and feel their experience exposed in every chapter. Best of all, Jeff does not just expose reality, he writes with a constant nudge upward. *Finding Our Way* will compel you to lean into God's highest call for your life and your church.

—TIM SCHROEDER
RCMP Chaplain
Author, *Life By The Hour*

Flourishing congregations rarely thrive by accident. Intentionality is central. In *Finding Our Way*, Jeff Lockyer unveils strategic steps taken at Southridge to ensure their evolving identity and activities moved in a concerted direction to get from "here to there." This book documents how Southridge blossomed into a church that partners with others to make a positive difference in their neighborhood, city, nation, and world. In the process their aspirations, values, and actions as a community of faith became clearer, grounded in life-transforming discipleship, home-based faith formation, leadership development, and innovation. In a Canadian context where many congregations struggle to effectively minister to those outside their walls or adapt ministry vision and practices to a global pandemic, *Finding Our Way* offers thoughtful and practical stories of hope that will assist congregations who aspire to flourish.

—JOEL THIESSEN
Professor of Sociology, Ambrose University
Director, Flourishing Congregations Institute
Author, *Signs of Life*

In *Finding our Way*, author Jeff Lockyer thoughtfully describes his journey as a leader in a local church. In the difficult decisions and the messy transitions, Jeff gives us a unique look behind the scenes of their work to date and the ensuing benefits of becoming a church that spends a disproportionate amount of energy and resources living out the teaching of Jesus by both serving and leading on the front lines of their community. *Finding Our Way* invites church leaders into conversations about the future of the church which will challenge and engage both thought leaders and practitioners alike.

—ROBB & LOIS WARREN
Executive Directors, Global Leadership Network Canada

Finding Our Way

JEFF LOCKYER

Finding Our Way

*Reclaiming the First-Century Church
in the Twenty-First Century*

Foreword by Alan Hirsch

WIPF *&* STOCK · Eugene, Oregon

FINDING OUR WAY
Reclaiming the First-Century Church in the Twenty-First Century

Wipf & Stock
An Imprint of Wipf and Stock Publishers
199 W. 8th Ave., Suite 3
Eugene, OR 97401

www.wipfandstock.com

PAPERBACK ISBN: 978-1-6667-2470-7
HARDCOVER ISBN: 978-1-6667-2031-0
EBOOK ISBN: 978-1-6667-2032-7

08/05/21

To my parents, Doug and Sue Lockyer.

Dad, aside from representing the bull's-eye of my sense of calling all these years, thanks for being the kind of parent who—even before devoting yourself to following Jesus—consistently demonstrated self-sacrificing love.

Mom, thanks for your tireless efforts to build faith and spirituality into us as kids—especially when it felt like you were carrying that burden on your own. Our faith and any kingdom influence we now have is your legacy.

Contents

Foreword

SOME YEARS AGO, I wrote what I consider my core contribution to the missiology conversation, *The Forgotten Ways*. In that book I called readers to a phenomenology of the apostolic movement. In essence I was calling readers—the church—to embrace the factors that would create explosive Jesus movements for our day. It was essentially a reminder of the DNA of the Jesus way. Since then, I have written several more books that reference back to this book and *The Shaping of Things to Come*, my foundational book.

So now, I read Jeff Lockyer's *Finding Our Way* and see how he too is calling us to live out the incarnational mission that God has called us to. Jeff speaks to us all out of years of experience, of walking with Jesus and with deacons and elders and congregants, seeking not to find the next best thing but simply to live out the Jesus way. He kindly reminds us that the formulaic approach where one goes to the next big conference and takes good notes no longer works. It really boils down to following the leader and struggling with what Jesus wants for his followers. What Jeff calls us to is simply acknowledging that Jesus is Lord and it is he and he alone who defines the core purpose and mission of the church.

You will no doubt wince at some of his ideas. You may get uncomfortable reading a chapter or two, but ultimately you will be transformed in your thinking of discipleship, community and mission. I've termed this element an mDNA and that permeates every page of this book. You won't be called to follow Jeff, or a North American business model, or even the latest fad but rather go back centuries to simply acknowledging and following Jesus. I dare say you won't be able to find a better model.

So, put aside your biases and differences and jump into this accessible, very practical manifesto that dates back to the early church. Whether a formal church leader or passionate lay member, enjoy the transformation. Embrace the risks. And wait to see Jesus—our founder—lived out in a vibrant, missional manner, dynamic for both the first and twenty-first centuries.

Alan Hirsch,
Author, Activist and Founder, Forge International

Acknowledgements

I FIRMLY BELIEVE IT takes a village to raise a family, and it takes an even greater village to raise the parents of spiritual families. A book like this isn't something one person writes, its creation is the combination of countless minds and hearts, and the story it recounts, spanning more than a quarter century of our community's life involves countless more.

Special thanks though, to Jeff Manion for your direct encouragement to engage in the discipline of writing. Your slow and steady faithfulness demonstrated to me that you can become an author without selling your soul to self-promotion. I literally would never have considered giving writing a shot without your example and encouragement.

I'd also like to recognize Wipf and Stock Publishers for giving this book a shot. Your commitment to publish based on the merits of content rather than marketability has given this story a chance to be shared. Similarly, I'd like to thank Don Pape for including me in his community of creatives (papecommons.com). Your tireless enthusiasm for this project and faithful commitment to the publishing process was integral to seeing this story come to life.

As well, thanks to Tim Day for your friendship and mentoring. Your advice to read more parenting books than leadership books—because, metaphorically, the church in the Bible is far more of a family than a business—was trajectory-shaping in my posture of leadership. Thanks for your continued encouragement to become a better person than leader.

To Southridge Community Church—and its predecessor, Fairview-Louth Mennonite Brethren Community Church—I hope these chapters do justice to representing your faith and faithfulness. Thanks for not only giving me a shot in ministry leadership, but for continuing to give me a shot as you've repeatedly trusted our team as we've charted an unknown future. You've allowed us as leaders to live the adventure of a lifetime.

Specifically, I want to recognize our teaching pastor Michael Krause, who began this vocational ministry journey with me on the exact same day and we haven't looked back since. As my "work spouse," you've let me see below the waterline of the iceberg into your life, where I've had the privilege to view the picture of your heart devoting itself more fully to Jesus in ways that have been worth thousands of your words. Thanks for watching your life and not just your doctrine closely.

Most of all, I'm grateful for my *real* spouse. Becky, I believe you're the most underrated spiritual influence in our community. Thanks for being secure enough in who you are to be okay living outside of the limelight and to carve out your own faith and identity as the spouse of a pastor. And thanks for helping me grow in my capacity to love. Your capacity drives our family and everything we're able to achieve. I continue to be thrilled to see where God takes us on this adventure, together. You and me, Baby . . . forever.

Introduction

Losing Our Way

YEARS AGO, I WAS invited to consult with the leadership team of a neighboring local church. They had launched a new church about a decade earlier, but after a few years of exciting startup growth they'd found themselves plateaued right around the classic two-hundred-person barrier of weekend service attendance. Apparently, they'd brought me in to help them discover why. I started by asking them what their church was about, which they could all easily answer with their slogan, "People. Partner. Plant." Then I asked them what turned out to be a far more dangerous question. I'd wondered what this slogan actually was—was that their church's vision? Was it the basis of their ministry model? Or were those words the key aspects of their current strategic plan? All I wanted to know was what role these terms played in the operational life of their ministry.

I was not prepared for their answer, and they certainly were not prepared for my response to it. One church leader immediately responded by saying that "People. Partner. Plant." was their current strategic plan, but another board member immediately corrected him by indicating this was their church's mission. The pastor then shared that this, more accurately, was their church's vision, the basis on which it was founded in the first place. As they looked at one another with complete confusion, I made the intending-to-be-kind-but-probably-inappropriate comment, "It sounds to me like you guys don't actually have a clue what you're doing." After a breath of personal reflection, each of them responded with a giggle of humility as they conceded just that: that these words on which their church was based were just that—they were only words; they had no functional role in the direction or operation of their ministry.

Some Have *Lost* Their Way

For some time, I've resisted writing this book. I'm sure part of it is my Canadian overdone false humility that objects to calling myself an author. For the record: I'm *not* really a writer; I'm a follower of Jesus and a leader of a local church. As I search my heart though, I know there's more to that aversion than mere Canadiana in resisting writing this book and sharing it with others. Our world seems to be increasingly dominated by "experts": authors, podcasters, and speakers eager to share their silver bullets for success. And as digital as we're becoming, there seems to continue to be only an increase in the number of books, resources, conferences, and movements devoted to subjects like church growth and health. As a pastor, I've felt the stress of Ecclesiastes 12:12 growing in me with each passing year, *"Of making many books there is no end, and much study wearies the body."*[1] I feel the dread anytime a teammate or congregant recommends yet another book for me to read. For sure, leaders are learners, but I can't help but feel like the last thing the world needs is another book. So, to all you ministry leaders who already have too much to do, as a fellow church leader, I apologize in advance for putting these thoughts onto your already-busy plate.

And yet, over the years, I've noticed a growing need among church and ministry leaders for a certain kind of support. Over the past quarter-century, I've noticed a growing angst among pastors and ministry leaders from a few different perspectives, whether they're able to articulate it or not.

The truth is: the group of church leaders described in the opening story is not alone. Some lack the absolute clarity to articulate what it is that they, as a church or ministry, actually exist to do. Others lack the understanding of the underlying why—why they're doing what they're doing. In both cases, these kinds of leaders find themselves going through the motions of leading ministry without making substantive progress because they lack some critical baseline clarity. The apostle Paul reminds the Corinthian church, *"If the trumpet does not sound a clear call, who will get ready for battle?"* (1 Cor 14:8). When it comes to the bedrock clarity of what a Christian church is, what it's ultimately intended by God to do and be and why it does what it does, regrettably there are some church and ministry leaders who—while part of Christ's kingdom—still find themselves lost in

---

1. Scripture quotations will come from the New International Version, unless otherwise noted.

confusion and lack of resolute clarity when it comes to actually articulating, advancing, and fulfilling their kingdom calling.

Others Have Lost *Their* Way

There's another group of leaders out there who, by contrast, are abundantly clear on what they're doing and why. Many of them are up-to-date and well-read on the cutting-edge trends. They frequent the most common church growth conferences and subscribe to the most highly rated church leadership podcasts. And, like many of those resources, they bring a laser focus and their passion is white-hot for one thing: reaching people for Jesus.

While all unique, these churches seem to have many common themes among them. They foster strong invitational cultures and are always eager for their next message series. Their worship bands are top quality and deliver not only the latest hit worship songs but can rip the top radio hits from time to time as well. Their dress code is casual—especially the preacher, who dresses in a way that's relatable. Many of these churches have built-in cafes and some even serve name-brand coffee. Lately, many of these churches have expanded to multiple campuses, some offering an online service or campus of sorts. Many of these churches are impressive in their respective communities. And, to many church leaders—myself included—these have become the indicators of effectiveness that we've aspired to.

The problem that seems to be emerging, though, is that despite clarity on the goal of their weekend services and excellence in execution, attendance in many of these cutting-edge ministries is in decline. Whether it's the pace of societal life, generational attitudes around faith or spirituality, or the expectations people have of a faith community, "cool" services just don't seem to be cutting it like they used to. This only leads to a bigger problem for these churches and leaders. When they refer back to the books they've read, or tune into the podcasts and conference talks they're watching, the celebrity church leaders in those environments continue to be succeeding. And increasingly, a growing number of church leaders are finding themselves unable to follow the example of the megachurch pastors that influence them.

This only illuminates the larger problem: not *who* they're following but *what*. Many of the leading-edge churches and leaders of today are implementing a next-generation strategy that was birthed in the mid-1970s. Modeling what is commonly known as the "seeker movement" or "attractional model," churches like Saddleback and Willow Creek contemporized their worship services in ways that were intended to be culturally relevant. Then, the next generation's leaders, people like Andy Stanley of North Point and Craig Groeschel of Life Church, figured out ways to once again contemporize their services to serve their specific contexts in *their* specific day. Much of this has represented seismic shifts in how churches function and has been used by God to reach people for Jesus by the thousands.

Here's the problem for a growing number of church leaders though: they've been so focused on implementing a church model like the ones they hear or read about that they've never really considered what it means to be relevant to *their own* culture. They're building someone else's church in their community. Worse still, the innovation of contemporizing worship services (which has been an incredible work of God to modernize the impact of Christ's church) was an innovation of the 1970s—nearly fifty years ago! So, not only are pastors struggling with implementing someone else's church in their neighborhood, they're implementing methods that were once innovative but are now a half-century old.

Because many churches have primarily focused on delivering what works out there and what has worked before now, they're not asking what would best work for their community today. And as they watch their attendance shrink, they have not much else to do but continue implementing someone else's way of doing ministry, instead of discovering what would work best to participate in ushering in the kingdom of God on their part of the earth as it is in heaven.

Many of Us Have Lost *the Way*

At the end of the day, though, those first two struggles pale in comparison with the ultimate challenge I believe the church is facing these days. Most people assume that where the church struggles is in its execution of programs and ministry. But these days, at least according to the data, the challenge is much deeper. Today, the church is facing a brand issue, struggling with its reputation, especially with those outside of it.

A 2018 survey done in the United Kingdom (a country with a very similar spiritual climate to Canada) revealed that 81 percent of non-Christians do not believe the church today makes a positive difference in the world. Asked to provide the adjective most synonymous with their experience of the church, 34 percent shared the term "judgmental" and 33 percent chose the word "hypocritical." Overall, the survey concluded that in the United Kingdom

> church leaders are often liable to overestimate the public's good-
> will toward the Church.[2]

The survey challenged leaders of faith communities to address their "PR problem."

Another survey done in the United States specifically polled millennials on their perceptions of the church. In this survey, 56 percent of respondents felt the church only cared about itself. Eighty-five percent said the church was hypocritical. Eighty-seven percent described the church as judgmental. And 91 percent of millennials surveyed felt the most common impact the church had was that it was anti-homosexual. When asked to select an image that best captured their impressions of the church, tied for first were a finger-wagging preacher and megaphone-shouting protestor.[3]

How can churches feel like we're doing so well when our reputation is so poor?

At one level, it ties into the previous problem. For so many of us church and ministry leaders, we're focused on making our Sunday service or program the best hour of someone's week, with the ultimate goal of growing the participation in our ministry. This event-based, attraction-oriented approach to church and ministry limits our impact because it prevents us from facing these deeper challenges of the church for ourselves.

Worse, though, is that it fundamentally changes what the church is. For many pastors and leaders solely focused on reaching people through their weekend services, their underlying definition of "church" flows out of the biblical root for that term, *ekklesia*, which means "the assembly of citizens of a city." At some level, it seems to make good biblical sense. But what's critical to address is that it's just not how the Bible actually describes the church of Jesus Christ.

Before the community of Holy Spirit-empowered Jesus followers became known as "the church," they were known differently, as described in Acts 19:23, *"About that time there arose a great disturbance about the Way."*

---

2. See "New Barna Global Study Examines the UK Church," https://www.barna.com/research/what-the-uk-doesnt-know-about-the-church, esp. para. 12.

3. See "What Millennials Want When They Visit Church," https://www.barna.com/research/what-millennials-want-when-they-visit-church/.

Before it was known as an assembly, the people of God were referred to as a "way," a way of life and a way of being in the world. Early believers were known by their resemblance to *Jesus' way* of life (who famously referred to himself as "the Way" (John 14:6).

I believe that's what's most lost in the church today. As churches, we're putting on good events and running decent programs, but people just aren't seeing the way of Jesus lived out among our people through their everyday lives in a way that compels them to do the same. When people of faith were primarily interested in and committed to living out the way of Jesus, they were credible, respected, and impactful. Yet today, in many parts of our world, in spite of our high-quality services and well-run programs, observers of the church view it as hypocritical, judgmental, and distrustful.

So how can our churches change this brand and impact? How can we reclaim the respect of the reputation of Jesus among us? As churches and leaders, we have to recapture The Way, focusing on fostering a way of life and being that looks like Jesus, far more than delivering well-attended programs and events. And rather than catering our ministries to alleviating the stresses and struggles of the privileged—often masked as "cultural relevance"—we need to both invite and operationally stimulate a way of life that increasingly comforts the legitimately afflicted in our society at the cost of afflicting the legitimately comfortable. The legacy and impact of our ministries need to reclaim Jesus' Way.

Finding Our Way

Like I already said, I'm no author. And I certainly don't have the for-all-time, single silver bullet for church effectiveness. But for nearly a quarter century, together with some friends, I've had the privilege of leading the church I grew up in as a kid and watching God tell an incredible story through it. And as we've stewarded the thinking behind how we understand local church ministry, a growing number of church and ministry leaders have expressed that they've found it profoundly helpful to processing their own way forward in advancing God's kingdom in the twenty-first century.

This book contains four main sections. The first articulates the biblical building blocks, where God's word defines everything at Southridge. Admittedly, it's pretty dry reading, but my goal is to provide clarity, not inspiration. There are countless church conferences and limitless podcasts that inspire with stories of transformation, but regrettably many church leaders still are left wondering how to reclaim the first-century church in the twenty-first century. I'm hoping this section provides you with a biblical blueprint that you and your team can leverage.

The second section applies that biblical blueprint to our local context in terms of specific operationalized ministries. My goal in outlining our ministry in this way is not to provide you with a model to copy—there's only one Southridge Community Church and there's only one Niagara Region of Ontario, Canada in which we live. Rather than telling you what to think, I hope I can help you and your team process *how to think* about your ministry in your context for this time. Personally, I'm tired of hearing what the church *should* do and am desperate to learn *how* it can do the things most of us already know it ought to do. As a local church practitioner, I hope our tangible example can save all of you at least some of the "stupid tax" of mistakes we've made along the way, where some wisdom from someone who's been there can prove helpful.

The third section moves past our local church's specific ministry model and into a number of common church challenges and hot-button issues where the church, for the most part, continues to lose its way. If the blueprint and model bore you, skip right to Chapter 9 and engage in one-off topics that can help you process many of our modern-day church challenges.

The fourth section is more of the third, only it addresses issues our church has processed less thoroughly and navigated less clearly. I only offer them up as real-time examples of how our leadership is thinking about these things these days, again to stimulate you in *how* you think rather than tell you what to think.

My hope is that the chapters ahead will provide you with a framework to create clarity and articulation of God's heart for your ministry, and that through them you'll be able to *find* your way. More than that, I hope the various subjects addressed in these chapters (which are deliberately short to be easy to read) will provide fuel for great team discussion among your church's or ministry's leadership for how God wants to use you and your church in your context, in the hope that they'd help you find *your* way.

Most of all though, I'm hoping that all of us would be inspired to band together like never before to take an honest look at the impact of the Christian church in the world today, and not be content with such an anaemic effect and poor representation of Jesus to this generation. I hope that we can, together, figure out more and better ways to strategically and practically do local church ministry in a way that stimulates a vastly greater degree of Christlikeness among our people and across our communities so the people around us would run to God instead of away from him. As church and ministry leaders, I hope we can find our *Way*—the *Jesus Way*, in our day and age—as we rediscover what it looks like to foster Jesus' way of life.

More than anything, I hope this launches us into an increasingly collective and supportive journey of *Finding Our Way* together. We know it takes a village to raise a family—and we know that's true spiritually when it comes to the church—but too often there's no village available for those who bear the parental responsibility of spiritual families. Especially in church leadership, it sure can be lonely at the top.

This book seeks to change that. Welcome to the adventure of *Finding Our Way*.

Discovering God's Way

From Consumption to Devotion

1

God's Vision

A Restorative Force

WHEN IT COMES TO unleashing the power of the church, it all starts with vision . . . kind of.

Most church leaders believe that the sun rises and sets on vision; that vision is the core from which everything else in your community flows. Vision has been defined as a preferred picture of the future that produces passion in people. Because of this, many pastors see their primary role as visionary, keeping the vision fresh and in front of their people. Vision-casting has become an art among church leaders because of the chronic challenge in churches where it's been said that "vision leaks." Of all the dynamics of church life, what seems to get the most attention is the power of a church's vision.

Often, the Proverbs are cited to make this case. The King James Version of Proverbs 29:18 reads, *"Where there is no vision, the people perish."* This seems to be the slam-dunk biblical argument for the necessity of vision—without it, the people of God perish! Many conferences and workshops fill up on the promise of equipping church leaders to cast a compelling vision. Many leadership retreats have been invested in mining, refining, and word-smithing statements of vision. After all, no one wants their people to perish.

What's interesting to note, though, is what Scripture means by the term "vision" in Proverbs 29:18. In other English translations, terms like "Word from God" (NCV), "divine guidance" (NLT), and "prophecy" (RSV) are used instead. Most commonly, in fact, the actual word is more directly translated—as in the New International Version, for example: "*Where there is no* revelation . . ." Do you see the difference? People don't perish if someone doesn't come up with a great slogan. People perish—or at least miss out on God's best for them—when God's vision isn't revealed as *the vision* for their church.

Here's the thing: when the Bible talks about vision and its deal-breaking necessity among God's people, it's not referring to a made-up, sloganeered, framed-and-hung-at-head-office kind of vision. It's talking about the vision of God as revealed through the Scriptures. Biblically speaking, vision more accurately refers to the revealed vision of God. For sure, vision matters. And for sure, it leaks. But the primary vision God cares about when it comes to his body and bride is the one God's provided in the Scriptures.

So, the obvious question that emerges then is: what is God's revealed vision for his church? Which chapter and verse do you prioritize to highlight and underline to organize your church around? If the vision for God's people is to be received instead of invented, what's the process for receiving God's revealed vision for his church?

The Monomythic Cycle

In our context, we've understood the "revelation" of God to mean all of Scripture: the revelation of the activity of God throughout human history as recorded in the Bible. So, our quest to discern God's vision for Christ's Church—and ultimately for our local church—began with surveying the whole of Scripture from front to back. To do this, we applied what scholars refer to as "narrative theology," meaning we viewed the arc of the whole Bible as a single story. Before doing that, though, we had to first understand how the arc of a single story works. For those who haven't majored in literature (which includes me!), we need to understand something called the monomythic cycle. The term combines the root words "mono" (meaning one or single), "myth" (meaning story or narrative) and "cycle" (meaning pattern or structure). The monomythic cycle is the single pattern or structure of a story. We needed to appreciate that every story, especially an epic narrative, actually follows a very predictable pattern or structure:

First, it begins with the *original ideal*. This is the "Once upon a time" moment where everything is as it should be. Soon, though, *conflict emerges*. This tension is what gives stories their plot. From there, the plot thickens as things go *from bad to worse*. In spite of efforts to resolve the tension, the tension only intensifies. At some point, a *surprising twist* emerges, where an unexpected event reroutes the trajectory of the entire story. This sends the characters into an *era of restoration*, where the problems and challenges of the story begin to resolve. And ultimately, the story ends at a point of *superior ideal*, where the "happily ever after" dynamic is even better than the "once upon a time" era. If you reflect on your favorite story, especially an epic narrative, you'll find that stories from *Cinderella* to *Star Wars* follow this same predictable pattern.

What you may never have considered before, though, is that the single most epic narrative of all is the activity of God throughout human history. And you may have never realized (unless you've embraced narrative theology) that the arc of Scripture follows this same overarching pattern. A good friend and mentor of mine, Tim Day, wrote brilliantly about this in a book called *God Enters Stage Left*, where he detailed the various dramatic acts of the Bible. For our purposes, I'll just summarize them through the structure of the monomythic cycle.

God's Epic Story

The original ideal is *Creation* in Genesis 1–2, where God's design fully functions as God intended. There, repeatedly, when God saw what he had made he declared it, "good." Unfortunately (like most narratives), that didn't last long, because by the third chapter of the Bible, *sin emerges*, and because Adam and Eve abandoned God's ideal, humanity finds themselves separated from God. The "bad to worse" era can be a little harder to narrowly identify, but essentially this initial tension increasingly intensifies throughout the entire *Old Testament*. After the fall, humanity seems paralyzed to address its own brokenness, and throughout the rest of the Old Testament—while God is certainly at work in Israel—the brokenness or incompleteness of humanity only becomes increasingly obvious.

Tim Day summarizes this era in four phases: the establishment of the people of Israel (which, at its worst, became, "if we can be good people who avoid all the bad people, we'll live faithfully with God"), the emergence of the law (which sadly descended into, "if we can just get clear on the rules— and build more rules to protect us from breaking the rules—we'll get right with God"), the institution of the kingship (which defied God's best, believing "if we can get a strong leader like all the other nations, we'll get right with God"), and finally the era of the prophets (which turned God's redemptive message into, "if we could just receive some harsh accountability when we stray from God, we'll get right with God"). These four phases of the Old Testament form the basis for the dynamics of toxic religion—a man-made process of attempting to get right with God and deal with the consequences of sin by our own effort and our own way. When this kind of religion becomes the order of the day, the result is predictable: the powerlessness and failure of humanity to fix the problem of sin we've created.

By the end of the Old Testament, things look bleak for God's people. They've divided, been conquered, captured, and are exiled. God seems silent. There seems to be no hope, because not only are they in a dark place, but in and of themselves they don't seem to have the capacity to rectify things and realize the beauty of who God intended them to be. Yet, like all epic narratives, when things are at their darkest the light of the surprising twist shines more brightly. And in our best Sunday School voice, we declare the twist of the story of God to be: *Jesus!* (Frankly, in Sunday school, even if it looked like a squirrel and walked like a squirrel, the correct answer was probably still Jesus). More specifically though, what is ultimately so surprising about the birth, life, death and resurrection of Jesus (from the context of the Old Testament) is that God intervened and, in his love, did for humanity what people fundamentally could not do for themselves. The surprising twist is the gospel of love and grace, fulfilled in Jesus Christ: that while we were sinners—hopeless to make ourselves right with God—God made a way for us to be forgiven and set free for a new life with him through the gift of Jesus Christ. The surprising twist is that humanity gets made right with God by God's grace, through faith, in Jesus Christ alone—not through the futile acts of human religion.

This sets off a chain reaction—following Jesus' resurrection—where forgiven believers receive his living Spirit and are united together into a new spiritual family. And this era—inaugurated in the New Testament, known as *the church*—aims to bring the life and love of Jesus Christ to the far corners of the earth. Where Jesus came as incarnate love in one person, God's Spirit made it possible for incarnate love to multiply and expand through many people, as the bride and body of Christ.

This leaves one final phase (or "act," in Day's language): the superior ideal. I don't want to stir up unnecessary theological debate among scholars who differ in their understanding of the end-times. Suffice to say, the Story of God reaches its ultimate culmination when the ascended Jesus returns one day to establish what John describes in the book of Revelation as, "*The*

New Heaven and New Earth." In this case, however, it will be even more magnificent than the initial garden of Eden, as renewed and resurrected followers of Jesus are united with him and each other forever. Since this era is still to come, Christians wait in confident hope and eager anticipation for the eventual return of Jesus Christ to fully complete his restorative work.

God's Vision for His Church

Aside from upsetting scholarly people with such a crude summary of Scripture, what was the point of recounting the Bible through the framework of the monomythic cycle? When you remember that the "vision" that matters to God—which his people cannot live without—is actually his revealed vision, and you then outline and audit his revealed vision through the front-to-back framework of the epic narrative of his timeless activity throughout human history, you find something I believe is very significant: that the vision for the "church" already exists in the pages of Scripture; that the church is actually a core part of God's revealed vision.

In God's epic narrative, there already is a vision for the church. More specifically, there already exists a God-determined role for his church to play in his Story. God's vision for his church is for it to fulfill its role in the era of restoration, effectively filling the space in history between the surprising twist of Jesus' life on earth to the superior ideal of his imminent return and establishment of the New Creation. In between those eras, the church exists—Holy Spirit-empowered and unified—to function as God's restorative force on Planet Earth, to be part of God's kingdom coming on earth as it is in heaven. That's God's vision for his church: to be a Holy Spirit-empowered and unified restorative force in the world.

Since vision matters so much, it is probably worth it to take a moment and call a time-out. Notice a few things about this definition of God's revealed vision for his church. First, nowhere in this definition does a place or event to attend appear. In our culture, people of faith are most commonly referred to as "church-goers," because the church has become virtually synonymous with a building where an event occurs, typically on Sunday mornings. To be a church person essentially refers to attending this gathering. And while gathering as God's people certainly matters (we'll unpack why in future chapters), nowhere does attending an event directly appear in God's revealed vision for his church. In fact, God's revealed vision for his church isn't a program at all; it's a people—a Holy Spirit-empowered and unified people. The people of God are the church. Church, from the perspective of God's revealed vision, is a people who are in Christ, not a specific program we offer.

Related to that, the second significant thing that strikes me about God's revealed vision for his church is the intended outcome: that this Holy Spirit-empowered and unified collection of Jesus followers would advance the era of restoration of his Story. The ultimate purpose of God's church and its definition for success are implied, yet often very different from ours. In our culture, "church growth" typically gets defined in terms of weekend service attendance numbers, as if the vision of a church is the same as a movie theatre or sports arena. However, filling seats with enthused people is far from the comprehensive impact Jesus intends to have in the world. Ultimately, believers have been left with the legacy of Jesus to usher in all the realities of the kingdom of God on earth (or at least their local part of the earth) as it is in heaven. According to God's revealed vision, the mandate of the church isn't to fill seats with people but to fill hearts with Christ's love and fill lives and societies with the fullness of that love incarnated. Those are two drastically different outcomes to pursue.

As you think about your ministry or church, what's your current vision? Maybe more importantly—for starters—where did your vision come from? Did your vision emerge from a book you read or conference you attended or podcast you listened to? Was your vision established through a process at an intensive leadership retreat, where a collection of leaders determined what you wanted your church to be about in your context? Simply put: have you reduced the vision of your local church to *your* vision?

Vision matters, absolutely. Without it, God's people continue to perish and miss out on the vibrancy of life he sent his Son to bring. And practically speaking, everything else about your church and all you invest in and operationalize flows out of your vision. But when it comes to the church, not every vision is created equal. And not every vision is worth advancing. In fact, the only vision that ultimately matters, according to a proper understanding of Proverbs 29:18, is the revealed vision of God through his word. And as you unpack the epic narrative of God's enduring activity throughout human history, you discover that God already has a vision for his church.

What is your church's vision? As you consider it, has your church invented its vision or received God's vision? Have you been committed to pursuing less than the fullness of what God intends his church to be at this stage in human history, or have you embraced the fullness of what it means to be a restorative force in the world today, multiplying his Holy Spirit's empowering and unifying life as you increasingly incarnate Jesus' love across your society?

For the church, it certainly does all start with vision, so long as it starts with *the vision* already revealed by God.

2

Christ's Mission

A Three-Dimensional Life

WHEN YOU CONSIDER THE revealed vision of God for his church, you discover a very different picture of what the church is intended to be other than merely a weekend event. Even though most people, both inside and outside the church, understand people of faith to be "church-goers" (implying that the church is a place to go), God's intent for his church is far more expansive and compelling. God's revealed design for his church is for it to be a Holy Spirit-empowered and unified force of restoration in the world. His vision is for the empowered, unified people of God to partner with God in ushering the realities of the kingdom of God on earth as it is in heaven.

The question that then emerges is, "What does that look like?" If the church is to be this Holy Spirit-empowered restorative force of believers, what exactly is it that we are restoring? This leads us to unpacking the mission of God for his church, not just his vision. At a technical level, where vision paints a compelling picture of what the future should look like, mission describes what that actually involves doing. Basically, where vision answers the "Why?" question, mission answers the "What?"

In our church's journey of *Finding Our Way*, we actually referred back to the monomythic cycle once again to determine what, exactly, we were supposed to be restoring. God's Story begins with an original ideal, which had been compromised by sin but was now capable of being remedied through Christ's work. So, we unpacked in greater detail what God originally intended before the fall, in order to give us a picture of what it was that we were supposed to reclaim among us and across our community through Christ's risen power. And specifically, we observed three interdependent dynamics to God's original design.

Being "In-Spirited"

Most obviously, there was a spiritual component to the way God intended people to live. He created humans with the capacity to relate in intimate connection with and reliance on him. Genesis 2:7 says, *"Then the Lord God formed a man from the dust of the ground and breathed into his nostrils the breath of life, and the man became a living being."* This description includes more than the biological function of filling humanity's lungs with oxygen. Specifically, the text refers to God filling Adam with the breath of his life. This refers to the imparting of the Life of God into the life of a human being. From the very beginning, humans were intended to function through the presence of the spiritual life of God within them.

This, as an aside, helps to start to make sense of the implications of the fall. When Adam and Eve were warned not to eat the fruit of the tree of the knowledge of good and evil, they were told that if they ate that fruit they would surely die. When they ate the fruit, they immediately realized they were naked. While I'm sure many of us would die if we realized we were suddenly naked in public, the physical lives of Adam and Eve didn't seem to be immediately taken from them the moment they shared the fruit. That's because physical death wasn't the most immediate consequence; spiritual death was. While their physical lives now faced their ultimate limit—and since then humanity has continued to function with a 100 percent mortality rate—the most immediate implication of humanity's sin was the loss of direct access to the life and presence of God in the garden. They died in the sense that they were now without the experience of the explicit life and presence of God within themselves, and in the world.

We continue to see the implications of this today, don't we? It's the story of the person who feels there probably is a God yet feels empty inside. It's the anxious person who can't find peace. We see it in teenagers chasing different pursuits to find their identity. It's the person at the end of their life who can't find comfort or hope. In faith environments, we often have a description for someone in this place (whether always helpful or not): we refer to them as "lost," maybe because of Jesus' three-tiered parable in Luke 15. To describe anyone in this condition as lost is so appropriate because in their sin the presence of God has yet to find his home within them. They're alive but lifeless.

So not surprisingly, this is one of the implications of finding faith in Jesus Christ, and one of the impacts God seeks to have in people through the work of his church. God is eager for people who discover his love, and the life-changing message of his Son to respond in faith, in part so he can fill them with his Life. Many times, church leaders offer the invitation of Jesus as an implication you can experience once you're dead—the offer of eternity with God in heaven—but the more accurate biblical truth is that God seeks to make spiritually dead people alive in the here and now by reconnecting them with the life source of his Holy Spirit.

This was one of the first and most obvious implications of the work of Jesus, evidenced among other places in John 20:22, *"Jesus breathed on them and said, 'Receive the Holy Spirit.'"* The result of the surprising twist of God's story is that people who'd been living life apart from the vibrancy of the presence and power of God could now receive him. They could now be energized and supported in ongoing ways through their moment-by-moment reliance on him. They were now capable of growing and engaging in a quality of life that was impossible before. This remains one of the core functions of the people who, having been empowered ourselves, are now tasked with participating in the carrying on of Jesus' legacy. Part of the restorative impact of the church is to connect people to Jesus, teaching them to live in an "in-spirited" way as they were originally intended.

Behaving as "Helpmates"

As amazing as it is for people to be able to be "in-spirited" again, with the life and activity of God through the work of Jesus Christ, the fascinating part of surveying the creation narrative in Scripture is that that's not all God intended for humans to experience. Aside from a spiritual dynamic to God's design, there's a relational one too.

Many church leaders are familiar with the declaration of God in Genesis 2:18: *"The Lord God said, "It is not good for the man to be alone. I will make a helper suitable for him."* Even though God had already breathed his Life into a human—and declared it very good—and sin had yet to corrupt anything, there was still something not good about an individual, flawless human. The otherwise perfect human being God had created, into whom he had breathed his life, was still alone—not spiritually but relationally.

There was no human companionship with which this created person could share their life.

So, from there, God created what the New International Version describes as a "helper." Literally translated "helpmate," this is the place in Scripture where God seems to invent marriage. Yet, from a theological perspective, he creates so much more. In this moment, God establishes the dynamic of human community, and in so doing he's declared the necessity of relationships in order to live the life he intends for his people. As spiritually empowered as a person is, God's design is that we live as "helpmates" with one another. From God's perspective, people can experience his life and love better together in close, supportive relationship with each other than we otherwise could alone.

Once again though, it's easy to see the implications of the fall on this core value of God's original design. Since the debilitating shame of the realization that they were naked, humans have experienced the shadow sides of relationships with one another. Beyond the loneliness and isolation of those who struggle to find quality relationships, we see division, polarization, competition, and manipulation running rampant in our society. The pain of relational rejection, betrayal, or abandonment feels often unrecoverable. The unfaithfulness of people towards each other ravages families, businesses, and nations.

The good news is that Jesus' forgiving and saving work both rescues people from lives apart from God and enables them to experience a quality of relating to each other that they could never know before. In fact, New Testament books like Paul's letter to the Ephesians emphasize the relational implications far more than the spiritual. After celebrating how Christ's work has made them spiritually alive when they were once dead, he goes on to write, *"Now in Christ Jesus you who once were far away have been brought near by the blood of Christ. . . . Consequently, you are no longer foreigners and strangers, but fellow citizens with God's people and also members of his household."* (Eph 2:13, 19). To Paul, his focus was not only on people experiencing the energizing effects of God's spiritual life in them. He was deeply committed to believers experiencing the relational impacts of the gospel and reclaiming their capacity, through Christ, to live as helpmates with one another, even and especially across lines of diversity, racial and otherwise.

So again, this becomes core to the mission of the church: reclaiming peoples' capacity to live as helpmates with one another. In addition to facilitating right relationships with God, the church's mandate is to enable people to experience greater degrees of right relationships with one another. Functioning faithfully in this era of restoration means helping people experience life in a way that's better together than if we were apart or alone. Part of the church's restorative mandate is to help people overcome the "not-goodness" of living life alone by becoming greater "helpmates" to one another, as friends and family in community.

Becoming "Caretakers"

Amazingly, that's still not all we see in the Genesis account of God's original vision for people. Aside from the spiritual and relational dynamics in the way God made people, there's a societal one as well. In verse 28 of Genesis chapter 1, God assigns the people he's recently made with a job description: *"God blessed them and said to them, 'Be fruitful and increase in number; fill the earth and subdue it. Rule over the fish in the sea and the birds in the sky and over every living creature that moves on the ground.'"* In the order of creation, God put humans in a place to rule over the rest.

What's critical to appreciate, though, is what God originally meant by "rule over." When he talks of humans filling the earth and subduing it, the original language uses the term for exercising dominion. Often, we can misunderstand that term, presuming dominion means domination and abuse of authority. To exercise dominion, though, is to focus on responsibility more than authority; it's a term of stewardship. God's vision for humanity was never for the world to be ours for the taking, leveraging our power over it. Rather, as stewards, we are to function as "caretakers" of it. God's original intent in assigning humanity with this job description, above the rest of creation, was for people to assume the responsibility for the caretaking of the condition of the world: culturally, societally, politically, economically, and environmentally, among other ways.

Yet again, though, it's not difficult to see the implications that sin has had on our collective capacity to live this out. Aside from the obvious abuses to our world environmentally, as a society we tend to magnify brokenness instead of healing it. As a result, pockets of people find themselves on the margins, neglected and unsupported. Tax dollars fund basic degrees of social supports (often inaccessible to the people who need them most), which enables people to treat the truly hurting in an "out-of-sight, out-of-mind" kind of way. Beyond ignorance and marginalization, our capitalistic society breeds injustices in many forms.

Once again, though, God's heart is that people of faith, and especially his Holy Spirit-empowered and unified church, would participate in righting these social wrongs. Fundamental to a life of faith in Jesus Christ is a compassion and justice that practically makes a difference in the needs and pain of our world. In fact, it's essential to living a legitimate faith in Jesus. James says to first-century believers: *"Suppose a brother or a sister is without clothes and daily food. If one of you says to them, 'Go in peace; keep warm and well fed,' but does nothing about their physical needs, what good is it? In the same way, faith by itself, if it is not accompanied by action, is dead."* A Christian faith—which can be automatically extended collectively to a Christian Church—that fails to visibly and practically care for the needs around it is actually no faith or church at all. Just as God assigned from the very beginning, believers are to reclaim their responsibility as caretakers for the brokenness, pain and struggle in their world. And, consistent with the Way of Jesus, Christ followers are to serve among the poor—and *with* the poor—as opposed to 'serving the poor,' as if from a separated position of privilege.

This then becomes a third critical mandate of the Christian church. Though government and social services provide supports in many parts of our world (but certainly not all), God's vision always was that his people would take responsibility for the brokenness around them. In addition to the reconnection of people to God and helpmates to one another, the extension of compassion and justice both locally and globally is a core component of the Christian church functioning faithfully in the era of restoration it finds itself in as a part of God's Story. Part of the church's restorative mandate is to take its place as the people in their community who are most responsible for the condition of their world and to actively engage in supporting and resolving its brokenness and suffering. Churches are to function as the caretakers of their communities through an active Christlike love that befriends and instills flourishing of those on the margins.

Three-In-One

One of the greatest mysteries of God is the theological concept of the Trinity—God's three-in-one-ness. Without presuming to completely understand it, in the Trinity the three distinct, individual, unique persons live in complete, indissoluble unity with each other. God the Father, God the

Son, and God the Holy Spirit each are completely and together, interdependently, three Persons as the One God.

When it comes to the mission God intends for the church, he intends for a very similar dynamic to exist. None of the features of God's original design are more important to him than another. And none can exist without the others. None of the features of the way he first created people to live are unaffected by sin, so all of these aspects are critical components of the Church's mandate in the world today. Some church leaders like to believe that evangelism—saving souls—is the ultimate (if not only!) purpose, of the Christian church, but from the narrative perspective of Scripture (never mind countless verses to the contrary), that's simply not the case. And for some church and ministry leaders, to reframe God's ultimate vision of the church as a restorative force instead of a weekly event, and then to recalibrate God's core mission as the three interdependent purposes he desires us to fulfill—all reclaiming his original design from Creation—requires quite a mindset shift. Is it possible that the "gospel" of modern Christianity that many of us have bought into is actually not the full, holistic gospel according to Scripture; not merely saving souls, but restoring God's vision for humanity and the world?

This becomes a pivotal stage in the journey of *Finding Our Way*. When we appreciate God's vision for his church to be a Holy Spirit-empowered, unified force for restoration in the world through Jesus Christ, and then understand that he desires his church to focus on restoring three aspects he designed in creation, we can start to see the full potential and experience the real power that Christ leverages through the church. We believe at Southridge that the full power of the Trinity can only be unleashed through the fullness of his three-dimensional mission on earth!

In our context, we've labeled these three fundamental aspects to our mission as "Inspiration" (not the hype kind but the "in-spirited" kind), "Connection" (establishing "helpmate" relationships) and "Action" (short for social action). Everything we do seeks to advance these three objectives. And each of these aspects of church life mutually and reciprocally supports the others in growing interdependence. No one aspect is more important than the others; they're all mission critical. Those areas of our church that are weaker at any time receive disproportionate attention and investment, in order for our community to be firing on all cylinders. How this then plays out in the life of our community is the next conversation.

When it comes to the vision of Christ's church, we need to be ultra-clear on the "Why?"—why God designed the church in the first place. To be faithful to that vision for the church to be a Holy Spirit-empowered restorative force, though, we need to be even clearer on the "What?" What is your church's mission? Does it encompass all three aspects of God's original design? More importantly: does it holistically and comprehensively foster the way of life God originally intended—that sin corrupted—that Jesus came to live, die and rise again to restore through his followers?

In the journey of *Finding Our Way*, maybe that leads you to ask the next question: "How?" Gaining that clarity is the next step in the adventure.

3

The Church's Model

The Primary Programs

THIS MAY BE ONE of the riskiest topics to address. These days, there seems to be a love-hate relationship with ministry models. On the one hand, some church leaders are eager to learn about and hear which models work best. They invest a majority of their time researching models and exhaust their staff and volunteers by constantly changing their models, re-jigging the sails of their ministry with every new wind of thought. Other leaders, because of this overdone reliance on models, have swung the other way and abandoned any attention to models whatsoever. They lead their church in a more "organic" way, preferring to deemphasize the structure of how ministry happens.

On the journey of *Finding Our Way*, I believe models matter. Jesus taught that it's important to put new wine in a new wineskin, so you don't lose it. In other words, how you package something can be almost as important as what you're packaging. The same is true in the church. That's why wineskins—or in our context, ministry models—matter, so long as you don't confuse the wineskin with the wine. From my perspective, defining your ministry model is an integral process to *Finding Our Way*. Where vision asks the "Why?" question, and mission focuses on the "What?" question, there remains a "How?" question. This question, on a practical level, is essential to clarify in order to fulfill God's intended mission and realize God's ultimate vision for his church.

So, the question then becomes, "Where do you find the ministry model after which to pattern your church?" From which book, podcast, conference or workshop can the silver-bullet model be found? In our church's journey, we again rooted our reflections in the epic narrative of God's timeless activity throughout human history, outlined through the monomythic cycle seen in Scripture. The original ideal of God's creation narrative in Genesis was the place where we could discover what it was God desired his church to be restoring: reclaiming a three-dimensional lifestyle of faith in Christ (through what we refer to as Inspiration, Connection, and Action as described in the previous chapter). However, it seemed like the New Testament description of Christ's church was the place where we ought to find a model after which to pattern our ministry. So, we surveyed the writings to New Testament churches, and specifically assessed how the church was formed and worked in the book of Acts. In particular, we paid specific attention to the snapshot of the church provided in Acts 2:41–47, where it describes the earliest incarnation of the Christian Church in action:

> Those who accepted [Peter's] message [about Jesus] were baptized, and about three thousand were added to their [the church's] number that day. They devoted themselves to the apostles' teaching and to fellowship, to the breaking of bread and to prayer. Everyone was filled with awe at the many wonders and signs performed by the apostles. All the believers were together and had everything in common. They sold property and possessions to give to anyone who had need. Every day they continued to meet together in the temple courts. They broke bread in their homes and ate together with glad and sincere hearts, praising God and enjoying the favor of all the people. And the Lord added to their number daily those who were being saved.

This was not the first season where we'd reflected on the Acts 2 church, but what fascinated us at this point—considering the context of the monomythic cycle—was that the very same dynamics that God originally intended humans to live out, according to his ideal design, were being demonstrated by this fledgling community of followers of Jesus. The original design of God in creation was being reclaimed by these believers, thanks to the legacy of the life of Jesus empowering them.

The Acts 2 Model: Gatherings, Groups, and Giving Back

First, we see the spiritual, or "in-spirited," dynamic of God's intended way of life being reclaimed. After witnessing the power and presence of the Holy Spirit descending on, and filling, the gathered community, in Acts 2:46 it says, *"Every day they continued to meet together in the temple courts."* On a regular basis, followers of Jesus assembled together at the temple. When gathered together, they basically experienced two things. On the one hand, they brought their sacrifices to the temple as offerings to God, what was known to them as the act of "worship." And on the other hand, they received teaching at the temple from their leaders from the word of God. This two-step of revelation and response, of receiving God's word and offering worship in return, enabled the two-way relationship with God to be stimulated: worship expressed love from people to God, while the Scriptures and Spirit expressed God's love to people. Just like breathing, this inhaling and exhaling of love between God and his people is how the in-spirited life was maintained and deepened over time. Through this regular experience at the temple, people were supported in their relating to God, resulting in a stronger connection with God and a more ongoing and intimate experience of his presence and power in peoples' lives. Basically, by gathering at the temple each day, they experienced a greater degree of *in-spiritedness*— the very Spirit's breath and life in them as God intended in creation when God first breathed the Spirit into Adam's lungs.

In the same way that God's creation didn't stop with people simply being in close connection to God, first-century believers also fully engaged in a way of life that connected with each other as companions and helpmates. Verses 44–46 describe, *"All the believers were together and had everything in common. . . . They broke bread in their homes and ate together with glad and sincere hearts."* In addition to regularly assembling together as a larger church family at the temple, believers subdivided into closer contacts with one another by meeting together in each other's homes. And through grouping in smaller ways in the comfort and intimacy of their homes, first-century Christians were able to experience dynamics in their lives and faith that they otherwise wouldn't by only assembling together at the temple. They were able to meet one another's needs, which presupposes that they knew each other's needs through sharing their lives with one another, thanks to a degree of vulnerability that is far more difficult to achieve in larger settings. Like Jesus, they leveraged the power of meals to stimulate a level of intimacy that large-group gatherings just can't deliver.

And through this process of regularly grouping in the safety and comfort of each other's homes, these believers reclaimed the dynamic of functioning as helpmates to one another, rather than going it alone in a way that God originally described as "not good."

In addition, Acts 2 believers took responsibility for the condition of the world around them. Verse 45 describes, *"They sold property and possessions to give to anyone who had need."* Core to their newfound way of life of following Jesus was a relinquishing of their privilege for the sake of the underprivileged. They voluntarily sold assets they possessed—and abandoned the status or security that came with those assets—to make investments into the pain and brokenness around them. As I've heard it described, they willingly downgraded their standard of living toward "enough," in order that others could upgrade toward "enough." And to be clear: these first-century believers weren't just offering gifts to God (though they did at the temple), and they weren't just caring for one another (though they did in shared lives). In addition to the spiritual and relational dynamics of their faith being expressed, the church was also active in expressing compassion and justice to those around them—those on the fringes or margins, whom society would typically ignore—in order to see their needs met too. In Acts 2, the Church demonstrated a reclaimed social responsibility for the condition of the broken world around them, as the caretakers and stewards of all creation as God initially designed them to be.

Modeling After Acts 2: The Twenty-First-Century Equivalent

As we surveyed Acts 2 with fresh eyes, we were fascinated to see all three of these fundamental dimensions of the way of life God originally designed—which had all been eroded because of the effects of sin—being reclaimed in Christ through this church. And we were equally fascinated by the way each of these expressions seemed to contribute interdependently to the early Christians' lives of faith, in the same way God originally intended. Through the Spirit, Jesus' risen life and power flowed into the church and reclaimed the way of life originally intended by God. And in this microcosm of the New Testament church captured by these verses in Acts 2, we see the Era of Restoration in God's story in an idealized form for first-century Jerusalem.

The question for our church then became, "How can we capture this dynamic in our time and place in the same way?" How can our church function on all three cylinders as a Holy Spirit-empowered, unified force of restoration in the world (realizing God's vision), by reclaiming the three-dimensional way of life that God originally intended in creation (fulfilling God's mission)? How could we function like the first-century church in the twenty-first century?

Rather than modeling our ministry after a notable modern-day church, we instead sought to pattern ourselves after what we see described in passages like Acts 2. In every one of these fundamental ways that the early church reclaimed God's original intention for their way of life, through Christ, we wondered: what could the modern-day equivalent look like for us? The result was what we now refer to as our church's three "primary programs."

Not surprisingly, the first primary program was patterned after the regular temple gatherings we see in Acts 2. This is basically what our *Weekend Services* seek to achieve today. In the same way that assembling as a large group back then cultivated the love relationship between people and God in two ways, our services seek to stimulate experiences of worship (expressing our love to God) and expose people to teaching (articulating God's love for us). Our goal, quite simply, is for people participating in our weekend services to discover how to relate to God better, primarily through those two aspects of the exchange of love. Our weekend services help foster peoples' capacity to live an increasingly in-spirited life, where through these larger-group experiences, they can grow in their capacity to experience God's presence and power in ongoing ways.

Equally unsurprisingly, we've patterned ourselves after the first-century church's frequency of meeting in each other's homes, as many churches have, by replicating a similar program in our context: organizing our larger community into smaller *Life Groups*. By subdividing our community in this way and allowing people to supplement their weekend service experience with a meeting in someone's home (ideally with a meal, or at least a snack!), an opportunity is created for a level of comfort and intimacy to be established that can lead to a degree of vulnerability and care that no large group gathering can deliver. As group members talk about the intersection of their faith with their everyday lives, people can live out the more than one hundred "one anothers" of the New Testament: encourage one another, offer accountability to each other, pray for one another, actively start to care for and meet one another's practical needs, and so on. More than anything, the formal connection created in these groups leads to more informal and ongoing relationship—visits, texts, and conversations outside of the official group time, which enables people to reclaim the dynamic of both having and being helpmates to each other. In addition to our spiritual lives, God is reclaiming peoples' relational lives through our Life Group ministry.

Thirdly, and maybe most significantly in recent decades, we've patterned our ministry model after the compassion and justice we see demonstrated in the first-century church, where people voluntarily surrendered their privilege to come alongside and meet the needs of those who lack privilege. In our context, we refer to these programs as our *Anchor Causes.* A lot more will be said about what they achieve, and how they're developed in Chapters 5 and 10. Suffice to say for now that, as a multi-site church, every one of our Southridge locations is fundamentally defined, not by the location of our building or our meeting time on the weekend, but by the practical difference in compassion and justice it seeks to make in its local community. At each location, a core societal need is being addressed through practical programming that has been developed to activate our community of local members to rally around that need. And as the Jesus followers in our community voluntarily lay down privilege—in cash, comfort, and conveniences—we're able to elevate the status and quality of life of people in our surrounding society who find themselves disproportionately underprivileged. And through the crucible of unlikely friendship, we aim to un-marginalize people by eradicating the "us" and "them." As our Anchor Causes grow and blossom, our community, to a growing degree, is reclaiming its responsibility as the caretakers of the parts of the world where God has placed us.

Clarifying the Wineskin and the Wine

At Southridge, these three ongoing experiences—Weekend Services, Life Groups, and Anchor Causes—have been described as our "primary programs." Knowing that many other churches around the world offer similar types of experiences though (many churches have gatherings, groups and ways to give back), there are a couple significant features of how we've sought to pattern our model after the Acts 2 church that are critical to understand, and ultimately implement, in the journey of *Finding Our Way.*

First, we believe that it's imperative that a church offers all three primary programs—not just one or two—and that all three are offered as fully-integrated aspects of the life of faith you're inviting people into. I'll address this more in subsequent chapters, but many churches (including ours historically) are primarily Sunday-service-focused and often rather anaemic when it comes to their operationalized compassion and justice. When it comes to what they've built, these churches' input is far weightier than their output. But in order to recapture the fullness and interdependence of God's original design in creation, all three aspects of the life of the first-century church have to be operationalized. Just like a college or university that develops its students in multiple ways—large group lectures, smaller group seminars, and practical on-the-job co-ops or work terms—a church can't afford to throw its eggs of investment into only one basket of core programming. In fact, to ensure all three aspects are equally and fully adopted and integrated into the lives of a church community, it's critical to disproportionately invest in the dimension(s) that's less natural to the culture, both the surrounding culture and the inherent Christian sub-culture.

Second, it's critical to appreciate the role played by these primary programs: as a means to the end, rather than the end itself. The passage in Acts 2 begins by describing how people who responded in faith to the message of Jesus devoted themselves to following him. The practical dynamics that are then described are merely expressions of that lifestyle of full devotion to Jesus. And, reciprocally, each of these aspects of their collective way of life also served to, in turn, further stimulate their lives of fuller devotion to Jesus. Like a flywheel, these practical expressions served to both encourage *and* express peoples' lifestyles of full devotion to Jesus. This is a critical clarifier, given it was a three-dimensional way of life that God originally designed for people to experience that the church is now intended to reclaim.

So, why is it so critical for churches to clarify their primary programs as the means to the end instead of the end itself? And why does it matter so much to focus more on the lifestyle of full devotion than the success of their programs? From my perspective, this is the ultimate crux of what separates where the church has lost its way from the journey of *Finding Our Way*, and the focus of the next chapter. I believe, in a fundamentally flawed way, that we've confused the ultimate outcome of the primary programs of our churches and ministries. And in the process, we've focused on our wineskins but forgotten the wine.

4

The Ultimate Outcome

A Lifestyle of Full Devotion

I'LL WARN YOU: THIS chapter will probably be the make-or-break chapter when it comes to you finishing this book. So far, admittedly, I haven't said much that may seem revolutionary. Embrace God's vision for your church. Pattern your model after Acts 2. Implement three primary programs that, interdependently, develop your people and help reclaim God's original intent for our lives. Organize your ministry around gatherings, groups, and giving back. Doesn't almost every church already do this? Admitting that this is the case, it's the intended outcome of the church's efforts in these ways that we need to focus on in order to truly diagnose where we've lost our way and, more importantly, to discover the root of what it will take for many of us, as church and ministry leaders, to start *Finding Our Way*.

Cultural Relevance

Around fifty years ago, a seismic shift in Christendom took place. At the time, the church seemed to be becoming increasingly irrelevant and insensitive to the world around it. Where its traditions fostered fondness among the faith family, a gap grew with the world it was supposed to reach. Right at that time, church leaders began to implement a heart for Christ's love for the world combined with business best practices in the church. Instead of starting with what Christians liked, they began to orient their activities around those outside the church, and especially those who would potentially turn to the church for spiritual guidance or fulfilment if the experience of church seemed relevant to their lives. This shift in orientation towards outsiders is what many call the "seeker movement" launched in the 1970s.

Quick disclaimer: I am personally indebted to the influence of this movement in significant ways. Specifically, the way this era of the church embraced the others-oriented, not-about-me character of Jesus and highlighted his heart for evangelism was inspiring. Many of the changes this movement brought continue to be legacies in our local church, including the use of contemporary music and songs, a casual dress code at a weekend service, and the high value of hospitality. The seeker movement birthed in the 1970s—and which probably peaked in the 1990s—has left an indelible mark on our lives and ministry.

Having said that, despite the motivation being the others-orientation of Jesus, the best business practice of beginning with the customer in mind, which defined the heart of the seeker movement, seems to have emerged a shadow side that has become a defining feature of the church today: consumerism. You can start to see its impact in the nature of how most churches' primary programs work and feel nearly fifty years later.

On the one hand, most churches organize weekend services that are designed to be, in the language of church leadership literature, *attractional gatherings*. They're specifically designed to appeal to "unchurched" people. Their goal is to create services that people who haven't experienced church (or who have been turned off by it previously) actually love to attend. So, the topics addressed in their messages, the songs selected and the style of music, the creative elements, and even hosting announcements, are all delivered from that foundational framework. They're fiercely protective of language that includes, and fanatically hospitable in the welcome they provide, from engaged greeters in the parking lot to high-quality coffee to free gifts for new attenders. The marketing and promotion of these gatherings is critical, especially on big holidays, in hopes of drawing in a captive audience to consider the message of Christ. The cultures of these churches are highly invitational, since seeing people invited to attend is the primary way the church fulfills its attractional purpose.

In regard to group life, a similar approach is applied. Groups are designed beginning with the end user. People are organized into groups according to their geography to make them convenient. They're organized according to season of life so people can relate to one another's struggles: single young adults navigate their stresses together, new families support each other, and retired seniors share their common challenges. Sometimes groups are even organized by spiritual stage, so not-yet or new believers can focus on more fundamental aspects of faith while more seasoned believers group together to move past elementary subjects and dig deeper into Bible study. All of this customization begins with the preferences of the participant and represents an approach to group life known as *affinity-based groups*. The goal, for purposes of convenience and comfort, is to surround people with people just like them.

When it comes to giving back, beginning with the participant in mind becomes a challenge. On the one hand, the amount of resources required to make weekend services appealing to outsiders, and then organizing them into such niche-specific small groups, often leaves little room for mobilizing people for compassion and justice. Occasionally churches plan short-term mission trips, in hopes of at least helping a privileged person appreciate how blessed they truly are. Sometimes churches will collect a special offering—to sponsor an overseas missionary or support a local care agency or para-church ministry—so that they can say it has a "missions" component. Often times though, when you consider the overall "pie" of how a church allocates its resources, after Sundays and small groups, there's actually very little left over to activate this aspect of Jesus' way of life. At best, messages are preached to live this way with a "go and do likewise" individualized and decentralized approach. Churches will intentionally gather their people, and group their people, but they will only *suggest* that their people should live like missionaries, instead of programming and operationalizing it in the same way they do for the other core aspects of a life of faith. That allows each church member a "customized calling" that suits their schedule and preferences. Compared to gatherings and groups, this tends to lead to merely an optional *token engagement* in compassion and justice, if any at all.

This is not just the way many churches function these days; it's the way our church functioned at one time too. So, as the saying goes, every time I point a finger at someone else, I'm pointing more back at myself. What was built on a combination of a Christlike others-orientation and passion for evangelism, combined with best business practices, has led to a ministry that begins with the preferences, conveniences, and comforts of the participant, which commonly plays itself out in attractional gatherings, affinity-based groups and token engagement in compassion and justice. Fifty years later, this is what our efforts to be culturally relevant have yielded.

Cultural Relevance?

Here's the problem, and the primary evidence that we've lost our way: what's been intended to be culturally relevant has resulted in a church that, in the past fifty years, has never found itself so irrelevant to its surrounding culture. In the introduction, I cited two of many surveys reflecting peoples' modern-day attitudes towards the church. When it comes to those outside the church, their most common impressions aren't that churches offer gatherings they can't miss, groups made just for them, and engagement in giving back where that helps them grow. Society's most common impressions of the Christian church today are that it's hypocritical, judgmental, and worthy of distrust (especially in regard to money).

Let's stare that in the face for a moment. How could such noble efforts—even rooted in the servant's heart attitude of Christ—lead to these results? How could such sincere intent translate into such destructive impact? In my experience of nearly a quarter century of leading a local church, I believe this can be summarized well by a famous Canadian named Marshall McLuhan, who in 1964 said, "The medium is the message."[1] The means by which a message is packaged and delivered actually sends the strongest message that people receive, far stronger than the actual content of the message.

Consider the medium of attractional gatherings. When the primary message of the attractional gathering is that this experience is oriented around you, the medium introduces people to a faith system that starts with them. More to the point, when the primary message (even beyond the medium) is to attract and invite more people, the emphasis is on evangelism (or at least invitation) at the expense of transformation. So, should it be a surprise that, to the outside world, most churchgoing people live profoundly unchanged lives—inconsistent with what outsiders instinctively believe to be Jesus-like—when personal transformation isn't the starting point for how services are designed?

Or consider the way affinity-based groups work. When the goal of a group experience is to deliver something that's convenient for you,

---

1. See McLuhan, Marshall, *Understanding Media: The Extensions of Man* (New York: McGraw-Hill, 1964).

comfortable for you, and preferential for your tastes, what message does a participant receive through that medium? They're reinforced to believe that faith starts with them and is all about them, and more specifically, that to be in close community means surrounding yourself with people who will make you feel comfortable in your faith. In this environment, to be different is a threat to the affinity-based-group-trained believer. So again, is it any surprise that the Christian church would exude a fear-based judgmentalism towards people who are different than them in behavior or even belief? How have Christians learned to believe that difference is so wrong?

Now think about the token nature with which many churches engage in compassion and justice. When the majority of its resources are invested in its weekend services—everything from paved parking lots to gourmet coffee to theatre-style seating to top-quality A/V technology—and only a small fraction is deployed for societal difference-making, is it any surprise that outsiders to the church feel that the church primarily cares about itself? Beyond overt financial scandals (which obviously hurt the church's reputation), what would inspire those outside the church to imagine financially donating to a local church when the majority of those resources seem to upgrade the privileges of the already privileged?

While the origins of the seeker movement of the 1970s were not only sincere but seem to be Spirit-led, I believe we've reached a tipping point. To build ministry on the foundation of what is best for the participant—for a participant's preferences, conveniences, and comforts—as others-oriented and even Christlike as it may feel, is fundamentally flawed. I believe the reason our churches today may still be "growing" (at least in participant numbers) while our reputation is eroding is because *we're building churches based on the fundamental value of consumerism instead of devotion.* Much of the Western Church today has been built on facilitating consumerism rather than fostering devotion. And even where the Church sincerely focuses on meeting peoples' needs, those needs tend to be oriented around the stresses and struggles of the privileged, rather than creating an impact that intentionally afflicts the most comfortable, in order to better comfort those most afflicted in this life. We've completely misdefined what it means to be "culturally relevant."

According to the monomythic cycle—and considering both God's original ideal and the restorative era where we find ourselves today—God's ultimate goal was, as in Acts 2, for people to engage in a lifestyle of faith by devoting themselves to following Jesus. God's design for creation was not patterned according to the values of consumerism, and the first-century church was never built on them. The way of life God first created, that Jesus enables to be restored through his Spirit, is fundamentally based on devotion to him, increasingly losing your life in order to increasingly gain Christ's. And the church's goal—as it realizes God's vision, fulfills God's mission, and implements God's model—is to foster a lifestyle of full devotion to Jesus. That's the outcome its primary programs ought to seek to achieve.

This is why I feel the Christian church is at such a crossroads: because we're building churches based on the values of consumerism but losing the reputation of Jesus in our culture as we do. We're building growing ministries while the reputation of Jesus is eroding. We're focusing on meeting the needs of privileged people more than propagating the legacy of Jesus in our world today. And all the while, we think we're being culturally relevant while the church is on a fast-track to ever-increasing cultural irrelevance. For us to continue to do church this way would be the textbook definition of insanity: doing the same thing while expecting different results. Something has to change.

Painting a Different Picture

What if our gatherings fostered a lifestyle of full devotion in the spiritual way we see in Scripture? What if the fundamental outcome of those who gathered was a greater degree of in-spiritedness, where because of their frequent gathering they more consistently relied on the presence and power of God in their daily lives? What kind of transformation into Jesus' image would be possible if people were discovering how to more regularly rely on him? And what would the watching world see if those who most frequently participated in those gatherings were also, in their experience, those who were most growing into the likeness of the Jesus they understood? What if our gatherings stimulated believers to live lives of greater integrity instead of sending the message of hypocrisy?

Similarly, what if our small group ministries fostered a lifestyle of full devotion in the relational way we see in the early church? What if groups were specifically designed to include people of difference, and the purpose of groups was to intentionally take people *out* of their comfort zones? What if the fundamental outcome was unity-in-diversity, where peoples' bandwidth for welcome and inclusion expanded? What kind of picture would those sorts of helpmates paint to the watching world, where there were decreasing limits on who could belong instead of the increasingly homogenous message that affinity groups send based on the medium of their homogeneity? What if our communities of faith exuded legitimate welcome and inclusion instead of being built on the process of rejecting those who don't fit the mold?

Again, what if what mattered most to the church was the societal difference it was making in its community instead of how many butts it collected in its seats on Sundays? What if the majority of its resources—rather than the leftovers of its resources—were invested in compassion and justice, not only creating a noticeable presence in its surrounding society but exuding a sacrifice of its own comfort for the sake of the marginalized? What if the fundamental outcome was for the members of a church to relinquish their privilege for the sake of the underprivileged? While everyone else defaults to education, business, or the government to solve the world's problems, what would the watching world see if, both personally and collectively, followers of Jesus embraced their responsibility as the primary caretakers for the condition of the world and its brokenness? What if the church gained the respect of the watching world by putting its money where its mouth was? Could a church function in its community with that kind of credibility instead of distrust?

And here's a bonus question for you—especially for those most passionate about evangelism, who may be the most married to the culturally-relevant, seeker-oriented approach to church that mistakenly leverages consumerism: What did evangelism look like in the first-century church? In Acts 2:47 it says, *"And the Lord added to their number daily those who were being saved."* To what did God add people daily? To a group of forgiven believers who, in response to the by-grace-through-faith-in-Christ message, fully devoted themselves to Jesus and his purposes in the world. To evangelize is not to attract unchurched people. And it's not to convince them to mentally believe a list of "truths." To evangelize is to include others in the adventure of a lifetime, as they engage in what it means to more and more fully devote their lives to Jesus—who lived, died, and was raised from the dead to forgive and transform them—in order that they might experience "life until it overflows" (John 10:10).

How do you do that? How do you build churches through primary programs that generate the impact of integrity, welcome and inclusion, and respected credibility instead of hypocrisy, judgmentalism and societal distrust? And how do you include seeking people in something outside their comfort zones instead of catering to their preferences and convenience?

If you're asking those kinds of questions these days, then you, my friend, sound like someone who's genuinely interested in *Finding Our Way* together. Let's develop our understanding of what that can look like in this next section—at least through one real-life example and experience of our local church, and discover how a church's primary programs that gather, group, and give back can effectively foster a lifestyle of full devotion.

Designing Our Way
Fostering a Lifestyle of Full Devotion

IF THE CHURCH IS going to fundamentally change its image in the world—from one of hypocrisy, judgmentalism, and societal distrust to one of integrity, welcome and inclusion, and respected credibility—it's going to have to operate differently. Specifically, we will need to re-frame how our ministries work. Are they driven by an (albeit sincere-hearted) "others-orientation" that starts with the preferences, conveniences, and comforts of the "customer," and leads to a medium-that-is-the-message reinforcing of a faith fundamentally rooted in consumerism? Or are they driven by the features of a way of life that God originally intended people to experience and that has been redeemed and made available by Jesus? And, more practically for church and ministry leaders, what's the difference? What distinguishes a ministry driven (even unknowingly) by the values of consumerism from a ministry that fosters a lifestyle of full devotion?

This section provides some concrete ministry examples, presented in the opposite order to gathering, groups, and giving back. I've arranged these chapters deliberately this way, not only because it represents the chronology of the story of God's activity in our local church, but because I believe it also represents the priority and sequence a church leader will need to employ in order to see such a foundational shift in their ministry take place. While churches will continue to gather, group, and give back, how that happens will have to look significantly different if we're going to change the impact the church is having on the watching world.

5

Giving Back

Anchor Causes

AS YOUNG CHURCH LEADERS working together as friends two decades ago, we were experiencing early church successes. Having contemporized our weekend services, we were seeing year-over-year-over-year growth of around 35 percent. We launched a second service and found that both services were filled in about eighteen months. In addition to limited auditorium seating, our classroom space was getting tight, and the parking lot was crammed—all the kinds of "problems" pastors love to complain about with their pastor buddies! So together with our Board of Elders, we were considering options for accommodating our newfound growth. Do we plant a new church? Merge with another church? Expand on our current site? The joys of a "successful" church leader!

The Game-Changer

Then one day, a friend of ours named Tom Loewen (who was pastoring at a different church at the time, but has now been a teammate at Southridge for almost twenty years) shared a book with us, written by a pastor from Little Rock, Arkansas. The basic question asked by the book was, "If your church suddenly disappeared, would anyone in the surrounding world even notice?" I can't tell you how humbling that single question was to me and my teammates. In fact, at the time our church was located in a rural part of Niagara, surrounded by vineyards, so when we processed that question together, looking out of the windows of our offices, there literally were *no people* we could even see around our church who even could notice!

I'll get into more detail in Chapter 10 about the process by which this happened. Suffice to say, this question not only stopped us dead in our tracks, but it also redefined how we would deal with our facility congestion issues. Instead of simply expanding, we decided to relocate our church closer to the downtown core of the city of St. Catharines in an effort to put ourselves in proximity, not just to more people, but specifically to people of disproportionate need in order to start making a more noticeable difference.

Moving locations enabled us to begin flexing ministry muscles we'd never activated in our people before, as we started partnering with nearby agencies who served the poor and marginalized. One particular ministry was called Out of the Cold, a local interchurch refuge for homeless people through the winter months. Out of the Cold activated different local churches each night of the week to feed and shelter the homeless, and our church, with its newfound proximity, was able to become the Sunday night site. At the end of our second winter partnering with them, the mayor of the City of St. Catharines approached us and asked if we would be willing to continue sheltering the homeless after the March 31 end to Out of the Cold; to offer shelter to the homeless in a full-time way. Knowing this was the bullseye of why we moved into the city in the first place, we agreed, and for more than fifteen years Southridge Community Church has operated the Niagara Region's largest homeless shelter out of its St. Catharines facilities, twenty-four hours a day, seven days a week.

But that was only the beginning of the story. After a couple more years of watching God continue to draw new people into our ministry, we were once again facing facility congestion challenges. By this point, the trend of churches going multi-site was emerging. So, we started to conduct public meetings about the potential of Southridge becoming a multi-site church, and to our surprise and delight, the first and most repeated question our people asked during these public meetings was, "What would the 'shelter-equivalent' be in these new sites?" Somehow, in a span of just five years, the defining feature of our church to our own members was no longer its worship gatherings or physical location, but the societal difference it sought to make. It was incredible to watch our people catch the vision of why we relocated our church building just a few years earlier.

The result was that each new Southridge location has begun with a specific community need it intended to meet, around which our community would rally. From the outset, these needs, determined in consultation with the local government, other churches, and existing agencies in these communities, defined the reason that particular Southridge location existed, and has become the unique identity of each site. Over time, we began to refer to these various missions as our "Anchor Causes" of compassion and justice. In addition to the Anchor Cause of homelessness at our St. Catharines location, we now come alongside low-income families experiencing food insecurity at our Welland location, and we serve migrant farm workers by fostering friendship with them in our Vineland location. Today, new Southridge locations would launch only after identifying the Anchor Cause for which we'd launch them. Our sites are no longer defined by the place you gather but by the difference each of them is seeking to make in their respective communities.

The most incredible part hasn't been the development of these Anchor Causes, though. It's been the opportunity God has presented us to foster a lifestyle of full devotion through operationalizing this kind of compassion and justice ministry. Specifically, we've discovered three incredible benefits from building Anchor Causes.

Extending Christ's Love

At first, we weren't sure what kind of value we'd be able to add to the homeless community of Niagara, other than a building and some meals. But over time, as our shelter program involved more of our church members, relationships started to form between residents and congregants. And we started to discover the truth about the needs they actually face. Personally (to my embarrassment), I always wondered why, in a modern society like ours, we even had homeless people. Didn't our tax dollars create sufficient social supports to address this need? What I began to discover though, through the crucible of up-close friendship with the homeless, was that the most common issue wasn't a lack of social supports, nor was it the ineffectiveness of them. In actuality, the most common issue that crippled the homeless community was their incapacity to access these otherwise available and effective supports. Whether because of addiction or mental health challenges, literacy or transportation issues, or the prejudice built into the systems themselves, many of the supports to the homeless were available but inaccessible to them.

As our community wrapped the caring heart of Jesus around our residents, we discovered that the church had a surprisingly integral role to play in supporting the homeless, because what many residents most needed was a true friend, someone who could also help them thread the needle through the social system of supports available to them. By providing rides, helping fill out forms, and searching for information on the internet, our people could make a significant difference in the lives of the homeless simply by becoming friends. In real life, we were seeing the power of the parable of the Good Samaritan, where in Luke 10 Jesus encourages his hearers to "go and do likewise" when it comes to extending mercy and investing yourself in providing practical support to those you see in need around you. With no official training or special skills, our community could shine Christ's love through the simple gift of friendship to the homeless, a power we've now seen leveraged in all of our Anchor Causes. We discovered for ourselves a truth many have learned before us: that poverty isn't a shortage of finances, but a lack of friendship. It's friendship that makes the difference.

Experiential Discipleship

The second benefit we discovered as we operationalized this kind of outreach was the impact on ourselves as followers of Jesus. To that point, all we really invited people into were the larger-group gatherings that talked about God and smaller group environments that processed what you were learning in those larger gatherings. That combination was essentially the one-two punch of how people grew spiritually in our church.

But one day a passage in the book of Luke caught our attention. In the middle of Luke 8, Jesus and his disciples find themselves in the middle of a storm while on a boat. Jesus is sleeping, so the disciples wake him up. He calms the storm and then goes back to sleep. And their response, as Luke records it, is this: *"In fear and amazement they asked one another, 'Who is this? He commands even the winds and the water, and they obey him'"* (Luke 8:25). For years this never struck me but upon a fresh reading I was shocked by this reaction: "Who is this?" The disciples had, for some time now, been exposed to a good amount of Jesus' teaching. More than that, they'd been hand-picked to join Jesus' own small group to process what they were learning in those larger group gatherings. These people had access to the best sermons and small group experience in the history of spiritual development yet were still at a "*Who is this?*" level of understanding regarding Jesus.

Skip ahead a chapter to the middle of Luke 9, where Jesus asks his disciples what people are saying about him. Some say he's John the Baptist, others Elijah or one of the prophets. Then Jesus asks them who they understand him to be. It says, *"'But what about you?' Jesus asked. 'Who do you say I am?' Peter answered, 'You are the Messiah sent from God'"* (Luke 9:20). Suddenly, one of Jesus' disciples is clear, confident, and precise. He knows exactly who Jesus is, and his understanding is spot-on. What happened between the middle of Luke 8 and the middle of Luke 9 that moved them from a "Who is this?" confusion and uncertainty to a clear and correct understanding of Jesus?

In between these two episodes Luke records this at the beginning of chapter 9: *"When Jesus had called the Twelve together, he gave them power and authority to drive out all demons and to cure diseases, and he sent them out to proclaim the kingdom of God and to heal the sick"* (Luke 9:1–2). What triggered the spiritual awakening and "aha" moment of understanding about Jesus was not another sermon or discussion in a small group. It was the active involvement of his disciples in the mission of extending compassion and justice that changed their perspectives and transformed their lives. Experiencing Jesus' mission was the most powerful teacher.

Science confirms this. It's what's known as experiential learning, or learning by doing. A man named Edgar Dale, who researched the learning retention rates of various experiences, generated what's now known as "Dale's Cone"—a varying relationship between learning experiences and the retention rates of them.

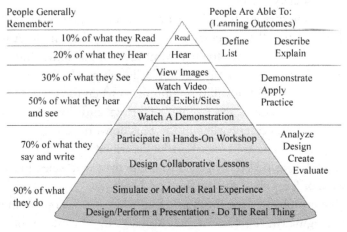

Dale's Cone of Experience

On the cone, you can see that people retain about 20 percent of what they hear, great news for one-directional communicators! That number increases to 30 percent of what they see (so showing you this chart is by definition worth 10 percent extra retention). Notice at the bottom of the cone though, that when they actually do what they're seeking to learn and talk about what they do as they do it, the learning retention rate skyrockets to 90 percent.

The point in all this? Experiential learning is the single best way to create "aha" moments of understanding. Arguably, participation in your mission helps stimulate your peoples' spiritual growth like nothing else can. As strong as your preaching or weekend service may be, the fact to face is that experience—by far—is the best teacher of Jesus' Way.

New Front Doors

As if that wasn't enough, we discovered that operationalizing compassion and justice ministry makes an extraordinary difference in how people outside of the church view your church. We should know this through our familiarity with Acts chapter 2, but I'd never considered this dynamic of the passage before, where it says the early church was *"praising God and enjoying the favor of all the people. And the Lord added to their number daily those who were being saved."* The early church did things that gained the favor of all the people that enabled God to incorporate more people into the church community as new followers of Jesus. What was it, though, that actually gained their society's favor?

Most of the surrounding society probably didn't gather with first-century believers when they assembled for worship in the temple. And there probably wouldn't have been too many outsiders in the home church meetings where Christians broke bread and fellowshipped together. I would argue that it was specifically in those moments when the church extended beyond itself—outside of the temple gatherings and home groups—that they were able to become visible to the outside world. And that visibility had an impact. As a pastor I once heard it described: it was their *good deeds* that created the *goodwill* that opened hearts to the *Good News*. Engaging in the mission of Jesus changes how the world sees you.

This has probably been the most remarkable surprise on our missional journey. Originally, we relocated our church to the downtown of our city because if we suddenly disappeared we felt like no one would even notice.

A couple years in, the mayor of St. Catharines approached us and asked if we'd partner with them to shelter the homeless. Now fast-forward a decade or so, a new candidate for mayor in our city campaigned on St. Catharines becoming what he called a "Compassionate City." Aside from the traditional government responsibilities, he wanted to change the culture of our society. When he won the election, he launched a website called compassionatestc.ca. At the top of the site he said: "My friend Tim Arnold from the Southridge Shelter has taught me a lot about compassion." The mayor of our city launched a government initiative based on the influence of a leader from a local church! That's a God-sized shift in church influence that only God could make as we have learned to give back in a far more than token way.

Friendship Makes the Difference

Today, our multi-site church is fundamentally defined by its Anchor Causes. Each of these Anchor Causes consists of some programmatic elements, but the programs are merely access points that stimulate relationships between members of our church community and those of the marginalized communities we serve. As those personal, life-on-life relationships blossom, we see God providing a kind of support and care otherwise unavailable to those on the margins and, since marginalization is ultimately a relational issue, fundamentally "un-marginalizes" them to the point where there no longer is a "them." We see spiritual growth like no other kind of ministry can stimulate. And we see new evangelistic front doors that people in our world seem more interested in than simply attending a service.

To appreciate how drastic a change this has been in our community, consider the comparison in resource allocation. Before we relocated our church, our annual operating budget invested about 80 percent of our funds (including staff, facility, ministry, etc.) into our weekend services, and the remaining 20 percent into our midweek groups and community life. At the time, we had zero dollars devoted to operationalized compassion and justice. Our only initiative was to take a secondary offering on Thanksgiving Sunday to support a couple of denominationally affiliated global mission agencies. Fast forward to 2021, where our operating budget seeks to invest 14 percent into our weekend services, 15 percent into groups and community life (including family ministry) and over 70 percent of our revenue into our local and global Anchor Causes (see Chapter 11 for how this plays out globally).

About fifteen years after being ravaged by that game-changing question, people across Niagara aren't nearly as skeptical about a church like Southridge when it comes to how they spend their money because they can see it consistently lived out across their community. Not only is our operationalized ministry fostering more fully-devoted followers of Jesus, it's helping change the brand of the church in the eyes of the watching world.

It's worth asking yourself and your team of ministry leaders: if your church suddenly disappeared, would anyone in your surrounding society really notice?

6

Groups

Love Beyond Belief

FROM VERY EARLY ON in my ministry leadership, I've felt a love-hate relationship with small group ministry. And the more I discuss their dynamics with both participants and other church leaders, the word that seems most common to peoples' experience is: dissatisfaction. People intuitively know their small group ought to be made for more.

Don't get me wrong. I'm a fundamental believer in the necessity of small group ministry in a local church. If for no other reason than the mutual-member care support structure, where small groups realize the Old Testament vision of Moses' father-in-law (see Exodus 18) to help both carry the burden and satisfy the needs among God's people for personal care. Small group ministry is essential to local church life. What I found in the early years of inviting people into the adventure of Acts 2 living, though, was a perpetual failure of our small groups—no matter how great the leader was—to deliver on what was promised. I've heard "dissatisfaction" defined as the gap between expectations and experience, and while we were inviting participants to connect in each other's homes for a quality of deep-spirited relationship they'd never experienced before, many participants felt burdened by the added relational obligation of belonging to a Life Group that often served to actually distract them from enjoying more time with their closest friends.

So again, in a back-to-the-drawing-board kind of way, we asked ourselves: what can a local church small group *actually deliver*? Or maybe more importantly—from God's perspective—what is the grouping of believers in each other's homes *supposed to deliver*? And, most importantly: how can a local church small group foster a lifestyle of full devotion, stimulating participants to become helpmates to a greater degree?

A Counter-Cultural Experience

What we began to clarify to our people, then, were the three foundational ways a Southridge Life Group could offer something they otherwise wouldn't typically experience in their everyday relationships. These were all mined out of the relational dynamics we see in Acts chapter 2, though none of which are necessarily unique to Southridge. They are simply the articulation of what makes groups work. One dynamic every small group could deliver was *a different frequency of contact*. Where most of our friendships have a sporadic nature to them ("We should get together again soon!"), and even our families tend to assemble primarily if not exclusively around the holiday calendar, a Life Group ought to be a consistent commitment to connect. Where most relationships get neglected because people are just too busy, the regular grouping of believers in each other's homes could serve as an ongoing opportunity to experience God's activity in life-on-life ways.

As well, we felt like our small groups could consistently deliver a different conversational content from our average interactions. For many people, the lunchroom or water cooler discussion focuses on the weather, sports, or politics. Mailbox or bus stop chatter with neighbors typically stays on the surface, and almost never delves into spiritual dynamics. But every small group could deliver *a different kind of conversation*, where deliberate discussions around the Bible, following Jesus, matters of faith, or the previous weekend's message could be debriefed. Beyond just catching up each time they met, the nature of the subject matter of what a Southridge Life Group talked about could distinguish itself from what's available through most relational dynamics in our peoples' lives each day.

In addition, small group members who met regularly and discussed spiritual matters could offer each other support. Without requiring participants, or even leaders, to possess formal theological training or a degree in counseling, members of a Southridge Life Group could enter into each other's worlds. Over time, they could share the deeper realities of the burdens they carried, and they could hold one another up in prayer support.

And, in many simple-yet-significant ways, group members could have each other on the radar of their attention by providing practical encouragement and support when needed. Where most people we interact with at the schoolyard or soccer field mind their own business, a Southridge Life Group could deliver *a different depth of care*. Group members could mind *each other's* business, entering in and extending practical support to one another.

This simple clarification of what a garden-variety small group in our church could deliver was a breath of fresh air. Not only did it relieve leaders of the burden that they, as the "pastors" of their people (as we liked to call them at the time), carried for the spiritual development of their people; it also freed participants from assuming their Life Group was a guaranteed factory for best friends, close buddies, and lifelong pals. And yet, by seemingly *lowering* the intensity of community that a small group was expected to provide, it actually focused and stimulated groups and participants around the core aspects of counter-cultural relating and *raised* the quality of experience that we could deliver. Through this programmatic playground, group members could engage in and experience a kind of relationship that, in most cases, was otherwise foreign to them and enjoy a different frequency of contact, a different kind of conversation, and a different depth of care. A few years after clarifying these deliverables, North Point Church in Atlanta summarized them far more appealingly than we were capable of, inviting their prospective small group members to *show up*, *join in*, and *be real*. Since then, we've tried to summarize these core aspects of group life in a fresh and succinct way as well, focusing both group leaders and participants on *eating* together (representing a regular rhythm of connecting), *praying* together (representing a spiritual focus to conversation), and *loving* together (representing the caring for and carrying of one another's burdens).

Something Still Missing?

At this point, we were beginning to feel like we had finally cracked the code on meaningful group life ministry, but something still gnawed at us. And interestingly, the more God grew our capacity for operationalizing and experiencing compassion and justice through our Anchor Causes, the more he clarified what was still missing in how we were delivering small groups. Over time, Southridge Life Groups were being viewed by participants as the relational "input" that counterbalanced the relational "output" of their Anchor Cause participation. Where people would embrace the risk of stepping outside their comfort zone to serve a marginalized people group, and then step further outside to get to know them and establish relationship with them, Life Groups were being viewed as places of relational refuge. If a group was growing, it consistently resisted subdividing because of the trauma of starting over. People valued the comfort and stability they experienced with each other. For new people looking to join a group, they would express a myriad of conditions and preferences for the group they would believe is worth joining, and often times we'd struggle to place them because of how closed and close-knit existing groups felt. People would refer to the church as cliquey and hard to really "break in."

Even though our small groups were being trained to engage in and deliver these three simple yet foundational features of counter-cultural relating, there was still an odour of exclusion and judgmentalism in our air. What was preventing us—we ultimately asked—from experiencing the fullness of God's love through our experiences of group life? What was hindering our community from experiencing and offering Christ's love with each other?

The short answer was: an under-appreciation of the value of love in Jesus and his word. It was through some biblical re-evaluation that our eyes opened to the absolute primacy of God's Law of Love. This is what Jesus referred to as a *new command* in John 13:34, the reorientation of everything around the primacy of love. I'm sure most of us are familiar with what the Bible says about love, but have you taken the time to really pay attention to the way in which the Bible actually teaches about love?

Aside from the nature of God being synonymous to love (1 John 4:8), we know Jesus affirmed that all 613 Jewish laws could be boiled down to just two: *"Love the Lord your God with all your heart and with all your soul and with all your mind.' This is the first and greatest commandment. And the second is like it: 'Love your neighbor as yourself.' All the Law and the Prophets hang on these two commandments"* (Matt 22:37–39). Beyond that though, consider the way Paul talks about love in Galatians 5:6: *"The only thing that counts is faith expressing itself through love."* Or consider Peter's encouragement to love in 1 Peter 4:8 when he says, *"Above all, love each other deeply, because love covers over a multitude of sins."* Think about the essential nature with which Paul describes the existence of love in his own life, when in 1 Corinthians 13:2–3 he says, *"If I have the gift of prophecy and can fathom all mysteries and all knowledge, and if I have a faith that can move mountains, but do not have love, I am* nothing. *If I give all I possess to the poor and give over my body to hardship that I may boast, but do not have love, I gain* nothing."

I'm sure most of us are familiar with the *frequency* with which the Scriptures teach on love, but have we considered the *primacy* with which it does? God *is* love. The commandment to love is *the* greatest. Superlatives like "only" and "above all" are used in reference to love, where to lack love is to have and to be "nothing." Have you ever noticed how love is described in such extreme ways in the Scriptures? Have you realized the ultimate priority of love in the Scriptures when it comes to the life of a person of faith?

Truthfully, we hadn't. But as we did, we recognized there was another breakthrough our community life could make, not only as we clarified the dynamics of a counter-cultural relationship that our small groups could deliver, but as we properly prioritized the outcome of love as their ultimate objective. As we made love the highest aim of our group life ministry, we were able to experience a second transition.

We were able to see the limitations of offering affinity-based groups and the underlying consumerism they were based on. Because of this, our church was robbing itself of a fuller and deeper experience of oneness because we encouraged and facilitated sameness. To truly experience the power of Christ's love unleashed through our church family's relationships, we needed to embrace the biblical vision of unity in diversity. Just as 1 Corinthians 13 (Paul's chapter on love) was intended to be a deeper explanation of 1 Corinthians 12 (Paul's explanation of the unity in diversity of the body of Christ), so we needed to deliberately and strategically facilitate difference among the members of our Southridge Life Groups in order to open the valve for love to flow.

The first stage of this was relatively easy. It involved diversifying Life Groups from initially organizing around a single stage or season of life. For the most part, singles were eager to connect and share experiences with people who were married and had families. Students embraced participating in groups where they could glean the wisdom of retirees. In turn, seniors enjoyed playing mentoring roles to younger people and families. As well, groups diversified across the socioeconomic spectrum, where more affluent professionals shared equally about their humanity with the unemployed, and where starving students blessed stable retirees. While still a work in progress, by slaying the dragon of homogeneity, our church family began to feel more like a spiritual family. Through the process of abandoning sameness, our community was embracing and experiencing the oneness that God intended, and Jesus enabled us to enjoy.

Love Beyond Belief

Where this tripped us up though (surprisingly at the time) was around theological matters. What we'd never realized was how much groups had established themselves around a common bias and interpretation of the Bible, and how incompatible people with divergent views could be to the life of a group. The more we pressed in, the more we realized how much "groupthink" actually defined our small group ministry. Millennials with contrarian views kept their mouths shut in groups galvanized around strong opinions, where conservative Baby Boomer groups had no use for alternate interpretations or ideas. What probably helped us see this default to ideological sameness was a growing polarization and division in our broader society, especially in the more politicized church in North America. For many of our people, to follow Jesus meant to align yourself with specific beliefs and theological interpretations, from which you formed a community of agreement and cultivated your spiritual "growth," protected from other views.

This then became the paradigm we sought to change. Through years of teaching on the primacy of God's Law of Love, we encouraged a culture that we now refer to as "Love Beyond Belief." This encapsulates a theological framework where the end goal and highest calling of a follower of Jesus is not to develop a perfect doctrine and unilaterally right beliefs (neither of which are actually attainable, despite all our supposed certainty and sincere conviction), but rather a fuller, richer, and more robust experience of Christ's love that is liberally shared with others. It's the re-prioritization of what matters most in a Christian community. Ironically, it is this re-framing of a theological framework that right-sizes the value and role of theology in the spiritual formation of a follower of Jesus. We've sought to embed in our culture the theology of "Love Beyond Belief."

This, then, has become our adventure in community life. As we're able to get people's heads around the primacy and superlative nature with which the Scriptures describe the pursuit of love, we've been able to open people up to a theological reframing. This reframing, in turn, is triggering a humility that is opening people's minds and hearts to divergent perspectives, which creates the possibility of growth, both theologically and in love. In the best-case scenarios now, we have people deliberately seeking out and forming community with people of contrary perspectives and views in order to make their understanding of Scripture sharper and—more importantly—enable their experience of love to be far fuller than they've ever known.

When the basis of your community life is surrounding yourself with other people who are just like you—who, more importantly, *think* just like you—you're unknowingly building a breeding ground for judgmentalism. Judgmentalism looks down on and excludes people who are and think differently than you. Love cultivates a humility that acknowledges the need to learn from those who think differently and leads to more radical degrees of welcome and inclusion. Now, as we're clear on the deliverables of what a Southridge Life Group can provide, we're deliberately cultivating environments that foster a lifestyle of full devotion to Jesus, reclaiming the helpmate dynamics that he came to earth to restore, by rightly focusing our people on what love requires, and strategizing around how to stimulate groups that express and experience Christ's love to a greater degree.

Are you clear on what your group life ministry can deliver? Are your people experiencing what they're signing up for in your small groups? And, more importantly, is the community life in your church accidentally sabotaging a culture of welcome because you're building cliques instead of communities? Are your small groups cultivating sameness or stimulating the oneness Jesus envisioned for his people?

The church will only be able to shift its impact from one of judgmentalism to one of legitimate welcome and inclusion when it re-clarifies what it's ultimately intended to pursue. As much as truth matters, Jesus didn't die and rise again to generate a legacy of accurate and precise belief. His Spirit's agenda is to propagate a love revolution. When it comes to community life in our local churches, people intuitively know they were made for more. I'm praying that your church and ministry leadership can embrace Love Beyond Belief to help get you there.

7

Gatherings

A Spiritual Gymnasium

SPOILER ALERT: I AM a hypocrite. And if you're professing to be a follower of Jesus, then unfortunately you are too.

For faith-based people, regrettably, there's no escaping that criticism, because declaring you're a Christian—literally a "little Christ"—immediately sets up the expectation that you resemble Jesus. The same thing is true for the collective people of God, the Bride or Body of Christ. To follow Jesus means you're aspiring to resemble him, but in our fallenness none of us will reach that destination fully this side of eternity. The inherent frustration represented by that perpetual gap reminds me of the Sunday School story of the kid whose mom constantly compared him to Jesus when he was out of line. If he forgot to clean his room, she'd ask, "Billy, what would Jesus do?" If he refused to eat his vegetables, again she'd press him with, "Billy, what would Jesus do?" Finally, exasperated and frustrated, Billy shot back at his mother, "I don't care what Jesus would do . . . I'm not Jesus!" That's the bottom line, isn't it? We're not Jesus. Not even close.

The good news of Jesus, though, is that he, by the life and power of his Spirit, wants to express himself in us. The wonder of Christ's death is that we can be forgiven and set free from the guilt and shame of our sin, but the real celebration of Easter weekend isn't Good Friday but Easter Sunday, where the reality of resurrection power sets us free from our ongoing slavery to sin. The essence of the Christian life, and what fundamentally sets it apart from all other world religions, is that the Christian life was never meant to be lived by you and me. The Christian life is Christ's life lived through us. Paul reminds his hearers of this bedrock truth in Philippians 2:13: *"It is God who works in you to will and to act in order to fulfill his good purpose."* The good news of Jesus is that only Jesus is Jesus, and he's eager to live his life through ours!

Abide in ME!

The challenge of the Christian life, then, isn't to try harder to resemble Jesus, but to learn how to allow his life to be manifest in and through ours to a greater degree. This is what Jesus was illustrating in John 15 with the metaphor of the vine and branches when he says, *"I am the vine; you are the branches. If you remain in me and I in you, you will bear much fruit; apart from me you can do nothing."* A fruitful life, resembling the life of the vine, is only possible by abiding in Christ. Reliance on his life and resources, not our own, is how we live in a way that resembles Jesus.

That brings us to a pretty critical question then: how does one learn to "abide"? What do you do? How does this work? Admittedly, the Bible seems a tad nebulous on such a critical subject. In his letter to the Colossians, Paul says, *"God has chosen to make known among the Gentiles the glorious riches of this mystery, which is Christ in you, the hope of glory."* Even on the best of days, enabling Jesus to live his life in and through yours remains a mystery of sorts, but over the centuries the church has laboured to discover how believers can increasingly develop an abiding posture in order to experience more of the presence of Christ in their lives and allow more of the power of Christ to bear fruit through them. Most famously, perhaps, would be Brother Lawrence's description of this process: practicing the presence of God.

That, essentially, is the key to living an increasingly in-spirited life, enjoying the kind of ongoing moment-by-moment spiritual connection with God where his presence can be experienced in our lives, and his essence can be exuded through our lives. I've heard it referred to as a practice-based faith: not a set of religious rituals to complete, but rather a vast myriad of possible exercises to engage in, to open your mind and heart to the activity of God in your life to a greater degree. A practice-based faith, one that enables a greater degree of abiding in Christ, yields a growing experience of his presence and an increased demonstration of his character as Jesus lives his life in and bears his fruit through ours. To reclaim the in-spirited dynamic we were made for, we need to embrace a practice-based faith.

What Do Sundays Really Do?

Here's the question we had to face as a church leadership though: is that what our large group gatherings sought to do? When we designed and invested in a Sunday morning service, was it stimulating a practice-based faith that leads to the increasingly in-spirited life that they were designed to accomplish? What were our weekend services really programmed for?

If I'm honest, they were a combination of a couple of things. When our church was first planted, we described ourselves as "A church where the Bible is taught and Christ is exalted," and that was precisely what our Sunday services were for. On the one hand, we treated our weekend services like classrooms, where we gathered to hear the teaching of the Scriptures. I don't want to minimize the importance of scriptural teaching or biblical literacy—and I certainly won't diss my ministry-long colleague and teaching pastor, Michael Krause (who's a terrific Bible teacher). What we've had to concede though is that providing a biblical message for people to take home and try to live out *on their own* was often seen as the primary offering of our weekend services.

The other framework we tended to operate in was that of a concert, represented by the musical worship of the service, where a fully revved-up band would rock out our auditoriums and inspire people to consider God's love, drink of his faithfulness, and pledge our followership for another week. Appealing to people's hearts and emotions, more than the cerebral impact of the classroom portion of our weekend services, these worship times ranged from high-energy to intimate reflection. Rare was a week when you didn't leave our weekend service inspired by the worship.

Those two results—*instructing* and *inspiring*—were essentially what our weekend services were designed to do. For nearly two decades we measured success based on our capacity to achieve those two objectives. There was just one problem: knowing things about Jesus and being motivated to follow Jesus often only ended up leaving attenders to figure out for themselves *how* to follow Jesus in the remaining 167 hours of their week. And, since the Christian life isn't ultimately something we live ourselves at all (but something Christ lives in us, as we are *"guided by the Spirit"* [Gal 5:16]), instructing people on what to do and inspiring them to do it left them frustrated, as they tried to implement their faith on their own strength and resources. Essentially, we were instructing and inspiring people to live a life they fundamentally couldn't. We were challenging people to live more like Jesus when only Jesus can live like Jesus.

Actually, there was a second problem. Because the medium is the message, these weekend service attenders learned, more than anything, to be just that: attenders. What they came for was something to be received, through what was provided on "the stage" (shouldn't that term reveal something's wrong?), and the sum total of their obligation (other than tossing money into the offering to pay for it!) was to simply take in the show. In a paradigm of Sunday morning that seeks to draw attenders, unfortunately you get what you ask for. You are stuck with a growing audience of people who wear the label "Christian," of whom the watching world rightly expects to look increasingly more like Jesus. But this is the one thing that is impossible for them to achieve because, even if they're trying to implement what they're being instructed and inspired to do, they're trying to do it with the strength of their own resources. And apart from Jesus living his life through them, they're guaranteed to be able to do . . . nothing (John 15:5). For sure, there are faith-filled and fruit-of-the-Spirit-bearing people who attend services at churches each weekend, but as they say, generalizations are generalizations because they're generally true. And what's become generally true of the church these days, to those both inside and outside of it, is that faith is synonymous with churchgoing. And as leaders, we're responsible for that result, because we've built services that are simply a show to be watched.

The Spiritual Gymnasium

Thankfully, we're discovering another way. I once interviewed Aaron Niequist about what he was learning about convening weekend services, and he used the metaphor of a "spiritual gymnasium" to describe God's intended function for a gathering. As soon as he said it, I was hooked. Instead of a classroom or concert, I feel like that image much better captures God's heart for why his people would gather.

In discovering how to increasingly abide—learning to practice the presence of God—there is a specific role for the church to play. The apostle Paul encourages his hearers to, "*Train yourself to be godly.*" Learning about and implementing the behaviors of a practice-based faith—in ways that enable unique humans to access the presence and power of God in their lives—is indeed a mystery. But it's also a process we can embark on, one that involves training. Training is about increasingly exposing yourself to productive repetition, but it also involves an orientation to exercises themselves. How can an aspiring follower of Jesus discover the power of reflection or confession, or experience the wonder of silence, centering prayer, or solitude without learning what these practices are in the first place? How can someone learn to leverage the spiritual potential of celebration or Sabbath, prayer, or fasting—let alone Bible reading itself—without being shown how? And more than just offering the intermittent teaching series or mid-week course on spiritual disciplines, how can someone become fluent in the language of a practice-based faith without being given recurring opportunities to experience how they work, and being repeatedly supported in experimenting with spiritual practices for themselves? More than instructing or inspiring, weekend services can function as spiritual gymnasiums that equip participants (notice the difference between *attenders* and *participants*) in their capacity to practice the presence of God.

Recently, this has been the subtle-yet-significant shift in the purpose of our gatherings. And the results have been exciting! Now, services are designed where musical worship sets reinforce spiritual practices. We've created programmed space in each service to be equipped in spiritual practices. And the majority of the followups to our teaching times imbed the intended biblical response in a spiritual practice. While we continue to model after the Acts 2 church by stimulating a two-way relationship with God through musical worship and his word, our primary goal is neither to instruct nor inspire. It is to *equip our people for a practice-based faith that abides in Christ.* And to do that, our perspective had to fundamentally shift from concentrating on making our weekend services the best hour of an attender's week to instead inviting participants to practice the presence of God in a way that empowers them to experience the most of God's activity in their lives during every other hour of their week. The weekend service, our primary program for an in-spirited faith, is now far more effectively stimulating a fully devoted lifestyle where people are learning how to let Jesus increasingly live through them.

Now you might wonder: doesn't the weirdness of engaging in these ancient rituals turn people off, especially people new to church? Aren't those moments uncomfortable for people, especially those who don't currently profess faith in Christ? At some level, the answer is yes, absolutely. But we've actually found that, when you "name the weirdness" and explain the experience as a spiritual access point, spiritual practices are appreciated by even those new to faith, because they help make sense of something they never grasped before. It seems that people instinctively feel like relating to God is, by definition, mysterious. So, they appreciate being equipped to tap into that mystery to a greater degree.

The greater win for us, when it comes to the discomfort factor, is the medium-that-is-the-message that engaging in spiritual practices provides. By naming that these kinds of exercises may be uncomfortable (but conceding stretches and intervals are too, yet contribute to our fitness) you fundamentally reframe what you're inviting people into. These days, we're unapologetic about declaring that our gatherings are going to be as uncomfortable as any workout at the gym, in order to deliberately take people out of their comfort zones and into the spaces where God's transformational activity lives. This helps recalibrate the assumed and unspoken expectations of people, who would otherwise relate to your church as a product to be consumed. By waging war on Christian consumerism in the hour each week where it rages most, Sunday morning, you help give your participants a fighting chance to activate legitimate life change by discovering how to receive the presence and power of God for themselves in a growing way all week long. By equipping people to live out an increasingly practice-based faith, you help believers learn to live in an abiding relationship with Jesus, where he's connected and free to bear his fruit through them.

Hope for the Hypocrite

Admittedly, the criticism that Christians are, above all else, hypocritical really stings when you've led a local church for nearly a quarter century. But I've never been able to shake the concession that it's far more real than it ought to be. For years I've wondered: how can that soccer mom be so enthusiastic about a worship service (and even post about their enthusiasm on social media) but then furiously swear at the referee at the game just an hour or two later? How can that long-time, Bible-believing Christian know so much about the Scriptures but still be so materialistic or gossipy or unforgiving? What's preventing such regular churchgoers from substantial and legitimate change? Why do people who attend church so much look so little like Jesus?

One significant reason is that all they're doing is going to church, because all their church is asking them to do is attend, to be instructed and inspired, but not giving them the opportunity to be in-spirited. By focusing all your ministry energies on instructing people and inspiring people, you provide them with temporary doses of Jesus. And, almost like a drug dealer, you train people to depend on the hit you can provide them each week. But when people leave those buildings and services—as well as all the resources invested into them, the staff and the programming to make those services instructive and inspiring—they're on their own. And no amount of instruction or inspiration enables a fallen human being to live out the essence of Jesus in their lives. Like Billy, we're just not Jesus. And we never will be.

Thankfully, Jesus is! And thankfully, he is risen and eager to abide in and empower the lives of every single forgiven believer to manifest his likeness in them by the power of the Holy Spirit. To do that, people need to be equipped in the behaviors of abiding. They need to discover how to practice the presence of God. And they require regular, repeated experiences to experiment with and be supported in engaging in a variety of spiritual practices in their own lives. Equipping a practice-based faith can enable a believer to practice the presence of God that allows Jesus—the True-Life Source—to bear his fruit in them.

With some subtle-yet-significant shifts, your weekend service can produce more than faithful churchgoers. You can develop people who increasingly resemble Jesus to their friends and family, their coworkers and classmates, and their teammates and neighbors. Just be clear: you won't do it through better instruction or more inspiration. Frankly, you won't do it through any of your own resources. You'll only do it if you increasingly equip your people to participate in the kinds of activities that access the presence and power of God themselves. Your weekend services can foster a lifestyle of full devotion through stimulating a greater degree of in-spiritedness as you focus on providing the training ground for a practice-based faith. By redefining your gatherings from classrooms or concerts to a Spiritual Gymnasium, you can help the watching world see "little Christs" who are continually growing. And even though, on this side of eternity, everyone who professes to follow Jesus will remain, by definition, a hypocrite, you'll give your community a chance to shine Jesus' character on others with growing integrity and help change the reputation of the Christian Church in your community.

8

Family Ministry

ONE OF THE BEDROCKS of a thriving local church is its ministry to children, investing in its next generation. Jesus certainly demonstrated a heart for kids to know his love—among other places, in Luke 18:16: *"Jesus called the children to him and said, 'Let the little children come to me, and do not hinder them, for the kingdom of God belongs to such as these.'"* Over the last fifty years, applying a customer-focus to a church's ministry has recognized that quality kids' ministry is one of the top priorities of seeking parents and families, so the profile of children's ministry has been increasingly on the rise. As with adults, though, what can originate from a sincere-hearted, others-orientation to serve children and families can quickly shift into being perceived as yet another Christian product to be consumed, where in some cases, children's ministry becomes the spiritual equivalent of dance class or karate. It's just one more program a parent can plug their kid into in hopes of bettering their child's life.

Considering how challenging it can be to shift the mindset of a participant in a church from consumerism to devotion, it's critical to start people on the right trajectory from a young age. So, the development of children and teenagers is a core component of our local church's life. More than that, we have to concurrently shift the mindsets of parents so that the discipleship of the next generation of Jesus followers, as with adults, is not reduced to a program you participate in (or sign your kid up for) but a lifestyle of full devotion to Christ. At Southridge, we consider Family Ministry to be as core to fulfilling God's mission of reclaiming a three-dimensional

57

way of life—as a means of realizing his vision of restoring our world to his original design—as any of the direct investments we make into the inspirited life (that we refer to as "Inspiration"), helpmate relationships (what we call "Connection"), and compassion and justice (what we summarize as "Action"). So along with these three aspects to our church's life, each driven by their respective primary programs, Family Ministry represents an equally significant area of investment that functions as its own department alongside the others. Over the years, though, a few key features of what Family Ministry requires have emerged. These form the basis of our focus and enable our leaders to differentiate between mistakenly reinforcing a medium-that-is-the-message of consumerism in order to develop our next generation's full devotion and stimulate spiritual progress in them.

Faith at Home

The first involves framing it as "Family Ministry" as opposed to children's ministry. As the seeker movement of the 1970s took full swing, attractional gatherings were supplemented with equally-engaging services for children. Far from babysitting while parents were reached for Jesus, the goal of these programs was to create the best hour of every kid's week. As with large-group gatherings for adults, though, people began to wonder how a child would be developed beyond the instruction and inspiration of that hour, during the remaining 167 hours of their week.

As churches considered that question, they also awakened to what most influences a child's character development. In 2006 Pastor Mark Holmen wrote a book called *Faith Begins at Home*, which shared research on the most influential people in a developing child's life. Not surprising, the top two influences were mom and dad. After that, though, the list was telling. The next most influential people to a child were people connected by relationships, like grandparents, and the first sign of a church-related voice didn't appear until around #7 on the list, and it wasn't the children's or youth pastor, but the senior pastor of the church. This research created an appreciation that the most significant influences in a child's life are their home. Thus, spiritually influencing a child to the greatest degree demands equipping the child's primary influences to do so effectively. This was a foundational shift in paradigm for next-generation discipleship, where the church no longer saw itself as the provider of the greatest spiritual influence, but rather as a support to those who are. Partnering with, equipping, and supporting parents in the 167 hours each week in which they take direct responsibility for their children's development has become critical to next-generation ministry.

At Southridge, the primary way our Family Ministry makes spiritual progress in kids and developing young adults is by partnering with parents to raise the next generation of Jesus followers. Yes, we have kids' programs as part of our weekend services (which I'll explain later in this chapter), but rather than advertising them as yet another product for parents to consume, our goal is to invite parents from our first contact with them into a partnership relationship. As important as it is to learn a child's name and develop a relationship with them, we seek to build a bridge with *parents* in order to get to know them and discover their family needs and parenting challenges. We regularly aim to resource parents and offer workshops and parenting-focused small groups to support specific challenges. Modeled after North Point Ministry's Orange model—combining the "light of the church" (yellow) with the "love of the home" (red)—we're committed to equipping the primary influences in the life of the next generation more than mistakenly assuming that church leaders are to play that role themselves. Partnering with parents has become a means for far more ongoing and lasting influence in the lives of children and developing young adults.

Crib-to-College Development

At the same time, we know a local church still has a unique and direct role to play in the lives of the next generation. So, when it comes to the responsibility that we, as church leaders, continue to bear, we've reflected on the question: what can a family count on us to invest in their child by the time they leave home? Can a parent have confidence that their child will become familiarized with the Bible? What "tough conversations" can a parent trust the church has introduced them to? What values is a church seeking to embed in the hearts and psyches of kids that will produce a strong foundation for adulthood?

At Southridge, we're increasingly able to present our answers to these questions to parents as we invite them into a partnership to raise the next generation. Over a number of years, our Family Ministry leadership—together with our church's teaching pastor—continue to develop and refine an eighteen-year discipleship roadmap of topics and outcomes that form the basis of the content and curriculum of what's taught in our programs to kids and students. Referred to as our "crib-to-college plan," parents can track with what they can expect our church will expose their child to as they participate in our Family Ministry programs. Parents can know how—and when—children will learn the stories of the Bible. They can know at which stages certain core theological concepts will be introduced and addressed. They can see when Jesus' Beatitudes or the Fruit of the Spirit will be focused on. They can know when more challenging or sensitive subjects like mental health, or marriage and sexuality, will be addressed. And, most importantly, parents can be concurrently resourced and equipped to navigate these conversations and provide their primary influence on these discipleship essentials.

Appreciating that we're not the primary influences in kids' and developing young adults' lives, as church leaders, we still didn't want kids leaving home, on our church's watch, not having been able to access the learning and development important to their faith foundations. So, by beginning with that end in mind—asking ourselves what a college student should believe about Jesus, how they should live like Jesus, and how they could abide in the presence of Jesus by the time they're living independently—we're developing a single, streamlined, comprehensive, discipleship plan. And what's cool is that it doesn't wait to start when a child is a teenager. When we say "crib" we mean it, as the plan even informs what we teach in our toddler classes—and, more importantly, why we're teaching it—so there's purpose and deliberacy even as we care for and spiritually support our youngest family members.

Age-Appropriate Devotion

Obviously, one of the reasons local churches continue to offer kids' and youth programs concurrent to its weekend services is because the subject matter addressed to adults on Sundays, and the manner with which it's addressed, isn't always relevant or appropriate to their understanding. What that doesn't mean, though, is that we want to write off a child or developing young adult's capacity to discover and experience the lifestyle of full devotion from a young age. Similar to the shift in thinking when it came to our weekend gatherings, we don't just want to instruct or inspire our next generation. We want to equip them to follow Jesus as fully, comprehensively, and devotedly as possible.

So, a third area of focus for our Family Ministry, as we seek to make spiritual progress in the next generation, involves exposing our kids and youth to the three-dimensional way of life that God originally created humans for, that sin corrupted, and that Jesus lived, died, and was raised to restore. Similar to the crib-to-college long-range view, but far more comprehensive than simply developing curricula, each of our component Family Ministries has mapped out how it can expose its participants to the lifestyle of full devotion to Jesus in their respective age-appropriate ways.

This is what most distinguishes our Family Ministry from a more traditional Sunday School or Children's Ministry model: we're seeking to provide more than just teaching. Equally critical in our development of young children to awakening them to God's love and the good news about Jesus, so they can establish a personal relationship with him, is the relational dynamic of experiencing community with other kids. So, the small group times when our kids are together matter as much, if not more, than the large-group musical worship and teaching times. More than that, we encourage all of our Family Ministry Life Group leaders to foster connections with their kids and group beyond the program time (always governed by the safety protocols of Plan to Protect!) so kids can appreciate from an early age not only that a life with Jesus extends beyond participating in a program but that community matters. And even at young ages, by collecting offerings for church-wide Compassion-sponsored children and writing letters back-and-forth with them, children are being exposed to the lifestyle of Action. Many times, parents are encouraged to include their children with them in their Anchor Cause participation, so our kids can discover the values of compassion and justice in their formative years. It's amazing how even young children can be formed through this exposure to all three aspects of the lifestyle of full devotion to Jesus.

By the time our children are in senior high school, our hope is that they're experiencing very similar primary program dynamics as their parents. Their worship gatherings are student-specific but are designed less to provide spiritual feeding and more to equip them to feed themselves by stimulating a similarly practice-based faith as their parents. We don't want to mistakenly create a medium-that-is-the-message with our students that faith depends on you. We want them to know that their life with Jesus depends on their reliance on his life and power within them.

Similarly, student Life Groups have become paramount to their development, not just to help further process teaching content, but to help form the relational dynamics of a Christ follower: discovering virtues such as welcome and inclusion, valuing diversity, speaking truth in love, and resolving conflict. Student leaders encourage the students to be supports of each other, so they can draw on one another's insight and encouragement for the common challenges they face. And our goal is that, by the time our students have graduated high school, they have been exposed to the awareness of the role of the gospel in bringing compassion and justice into our world and aligned with Southridge's Anchor Causes. By the time a developing child is in high school, we want them to be clear that it's followers of Jesus who bear responsibility for caring for the condition of the brokenness of our world. And we want it to be equally clear to them that the way of life Jesus invites us into is one of increasingly relinquishing privilege, in a way where legitimately afflicted people are comforted to the affliction of the legitimately comfortable. So progressively, kids and youth are increasingly exposed to opportunities to engage in the lifestyle of full devotion as they approach adulthood.

What About Young Adults?

Often times, local church Family Ministries will include a separate set of programs specifically for young adults, college or new career-aged adults who, emerging in their independence, are still finding themselves in many ways. At Southridge, we offer an annual Young Adult retreat, early in the fall to help students from the local colleges and university to relationally connect with each other and our church. And at times we've made specific college-aged ministry available, like study cafés to connect and support each other during exam periods. But generally speaking, we've been averse to launching or building a more fully orbed young adults' component to our Family Ministry.

There are two main reasons for this approach. First, we don't want to segregate young adults unnecessarily from the full experience of unity-in-diversity we can enjoy as a church family (as we discussed in Chapter 6). Collegiate singles provide just as vital a voice as a retired grandparent in the life of our community, so our goal, where possible, is to integrate these young adults into our "regular" Life Group system rather than create young adult-specific groups of their own.

Second, by the time a person is a young adult, we believe that, while still young, they *are* an adult. And we value their contribution to the life of our community in our primary programs that foster our lifestyle of full devotion to Christ for our whole church. We want to include their gifts in cultivating our whole church family's in-spiritedness. We need them to enable our whole church to become better helpmates. And we're eager to activate their passion for justice as key players in our Anchor Causes. Not to mention, we have a history of viewing the emerging generation as the future of our church's leadership and want to integrate them into the life and leadership of local church ministry right away. (See Chapter 12 for more detail on how that process has worked in our context.)

Family Matters!

To us, Family Ministry is more than creating the most exciting hour of every kid's week. And it's far more than a marketing ploy to convince parents to give your church a chance. To be a local church that's fostering a lifestyle of full devotion as a whole church family, you have to, like Jesus, embrace the children among you. But you have to be clear that no amount of effort or creativity by a local church can supplant the primary influence of parents and caregivers, and if you want to make the greatest difference in kids' lives, you'll provide the best equipping to the greatest influencers by partnering with them. When it comes to the direct responsibility of a local church, you have to begin with the end in mind and work backwards, establishing a long-range view of your discipleship plan. And, preparing for adulthood, you want to increasingly expose children and developing young adults to the primary programs and the three-dimensional lifestyle you're seeking to foster, so that, as they enter adulthood, your church's definition of a life of faith isn't a surprise to them.

For generations, kids' and student ministries have been built on the wisdom of Proverbs 22:6 (NKJV), *"Train up a child in the way he should go, and when he is old he will not depart from it."* A vast majority of people still make faith decisions before their eighteenth birthday, so launching kids and developing young adults on a good trajectory is critical. But Family Ministry can be so much more than the development of the next generation. As you enable the next generation to engage in a lifestyle of full devotion to Jesus, a lifestyle that seeks to turn hypocrisy into integrity, judgmentalism into legitimate welcome and inclusion, and distrust into respected credibility, your Family Ministry can become the breeding ground for a church that changes the world.

Developing Our Way
Modern-Day Challenges

IN ORDER TO RECLAIM the way of life that God intended—the one that Jesus taught and modeled, and then rose from the grave to offer to his followers by his Spirit—the church needs to root its primary programs of gatherings, groups, and giving back in the values of devotion instead of consumerism. Each primary program needs to begin with that end in mind: how is it uniquely intended to contribute to a fully devoted lifestyle as God designed? And each primary program needs to be operationalized, built with leadership, systems, and processes to mobilize that aspect of the way of life of Jesus.

As each primary program—interdependently along with the others—contributes uniquely to fostering a lifestyle of full devotion to Jesus, people can experience their God-intended capacity to live in-spirited lives with God, as helpmates with each other, who assume their position of responsibility for the condition of the world around them, particularly its areas of brokenness. As this happens, the church can start making inroads on its reputation among the watching world, trading hypocrisy for integrity, judgmentalism for welcome and inclusion, and distrustfulness for respected credibility, because it's driving a faith based on devotion rather than consumption.

This is the essence of what I believe it takes for the Christian church to *Find Our Way*. Yet at the same time, there are other pressing issues and challenges the church faces in today's culture. These are often extensions of, but not limited to, the values of the primary programs of a local church's ministry. This next section seeks to address a handful of these most pressing topics head-on from the experience of our local church. Not every chapter will be equally relevant to every reader, but for many leaders, these challenges represent areas of local church life where we most struggle to *Find Our Way* in creating faith communities that clearly and comprehensively express the life and love of Jesus Christ to the world around us.

9

Multi-Site Structure

I BELIEVE THE CHURCH, most fundamentally, is intended by God to be the Spirit-empowered and unified continuation of the incarnational life and love of Jesus Christ in the world. It's not a building and it's not a budget. It's not programs or events. In spite of embracing that more organic ethos of the church though, I also fundamentally believe that systems and structure matter in the church. In fact, I would argue that they're a core part of how our Creator God works effectively.

Think, for example, of the creation narrative itself. It describes how God created a solar *system*. And each day he carefully built and developed an eco*system*. Consider his design of humanity, his prized creation, complete with its skeletal *system*, its muscular *system*, its cardiovascular *system*, or its central nervous *system*. Now consider the church, referred to in the New Testament as the body of Christ, where its members are compared to the individual parts of a physical body. Shouldn't structure matter in the one system that matters most to God? Remember the teaching of Jesus, *"New wine must be stored in new wineskins."* Even though the wine matters most, wineskins are essential to the life, health, and vibrancy of any local church.

Organizing the 3D Lifestyle

The question, then, is: how should a local church that's seeking to foster a lifestyle of full devotion to Jesus—in Inspiration, Connection, and Action, as well as for families—be structured? In our context, we've applied two simple values to establish an effective and expandable organizational structure to our operationalized ministry.

The first value is that *form follows function*. Simply put: we try to organize around what it is we're trying to do. Since we're seeking to foster a lifestyle of full devotion in 3 + 1 ways, there are . . . five departments! Hopefully, it's not quite that confusing.

Each of our core areas of ministry operates as its own department, each driving a primary program that serves to express and stimulate the lifestyle of full devotion. At Southridge, we have an Inspiration department (driving our weekend services), a Connection department (driving our Life Groups and community life) and an Action department (driving our local and global Anchor Causes). As well, we have a Family Ministry department, which seeks to (as described in detail in Chapter 8) equip children and developing young adults in the three-dimensional lifestyle of full devotion in age-appropriate ways interdependently in cooperation with the other departments. This keeps everything pretty straightforward.

In addition, we've removed the obligation for each department to run its own administrative and operational logistics and created a fifth department devoted to serving and supporting these other four departments with its niche-specific expertise. Called Ministry Services (deliberately, as opposed to "Church Operations"), this department provides the infrastructural supports to directly serve the other departments (where the other departments focus on and serve people), including facility management, finance, HR, IT, and communications. So Southridge is organized into five departments because, at its simplest level, there are five things we're trying organizationally to do. This also plays out in the organization of things like our operating budget and office spaces. We're seeking for our form to follow our function.

The second value is that we're *fanatically collaborative*: that everything we do is done together as a team. This is intended to protect us from silos and passion-based ministries from competing against each other, since we're seeking for the church to function as one body, not as many parts. We find the New Testament example of the early church's leadership compelling in this way, when in their first decision reported in Acts 15:28 it says, *"It seemed good to the Holy Spirit and to us. . . ."* At Southridge, similarly, we want every decision to be made with the Spirit, by an "us" as opposed to any one solo leader. Embracing the cliché that "together everyone accomplishes more," we want our ministry to be done as a team.

So practically, all of our various ministry areas work as teams—whether they're worship teams, student ministry leadership teams, or medical clinic teams at an Anchor Cause. Each team has an identified leader, and the collection of these leaders form departmental teams. In our context and scale, the majority of the leaders in departmental teams are now paid staff. Each of these five major departmental teams, in turn, has a designated leader who together serve to integrate the various aspects of our ministry into a whole church operation as a Leadership Team. Our Leadership Team, again with a designated leader (our lead pastor), in turn relates to a team that provides our operational management with governance oversight. This team of ultimate authority and responsibility for the health and direction of the whole church (notice again, it's not reduced to any one single individual) is our church's Board of Elders.

One Church in Multiple Locations

That may sound simple (because it's intended to be!), but when you start expanding and subdividing into multiple sites and locations—and, in our case, when each church location is primarily defined by its operationalized compassion and justice initiative in its Anchor Cause—things can get complicated quickly. Working with some great consultants before we transitioned to a multi-site model, we discovered that local churches could opt for a range of ways to organize themselves in a multi-site capacity, from highly centralized (like a head office with franchises) to highly decentralized (like a family of independently-planted churches). Where you land on that spectrum, we learned, depends on your values, bias, and the uniqueness of your ministry. In our case, we've tried to clarify our multi-site values to keep things as simple as possible.

No matter what size or scale we operate at, we want to organize in three foundational ways. First, we always want to *centralize expertise*. Where quality and niche-specific gifting matters, we want to streamline our church around the very best gifts available. This means that we centralize things like our weekend teaching and financial management, as opposed to insisting each Southridge location find or develop its own competencies in these regards. This is why we've retained a fivefold departmental organization even as we've expanded to multi-site, because the vision and strategic development of each of these core objectives of our church's ministry would be significantly diluted if it needed to be replicated at each individual location.

On the other hand, though, our second value is—whenever possible—to *personalize care*. The best part of a multi-site church is the way it can optimize the best of both worlds, leveraging the upsides of both a larger and smaller church. The upside of a larger church is its centralized expertise, but the upside of a smaller church is its personal touch. In this way, our locations have allowed us to retain far more of a small church feel that, at least in a suburban context like the Niagara Region, tends to be appreciated and trusted more than an overly corporate larger culture. So, particularly with our location pastors, whose primary role is to be the "face of the place" that facilitates personal connection and care, we encourage anything that's highly relational to be viewed through the site-specific lens.

That's especially true when it comes to the "friendship that makes a difference" in the operationalized compassion and justice of our Anchor Causes. Considering that each of our Southridge locations actually focuses on a unique societal need, we also have to *customize outreach* to ensure that our systems and strategies effectively serve the people we're seeking to serve. The organizational approach to a twenty-four-seven, 365-day home-less shelter is very different from a seasonal focus on migrant farm workers. A kitchen-based ministry to at-risk families experiencing food insecurity organizes very differently than a Life Group "adopt-a-farm" approach. So not only do these Anchor Causes need to be decentralized so they're oper-ating specific to their location, they also need to be organized in unique and specific ways that are customized to the needs and the fostering of unlikely friendships that can meet them.

The bottom line is that, when it comes to organizational structure, Southridge functions as a matrix-style organization. Every staff leader, and ministry they serve, primarily identifies with their department; that is, they have a "solid line" reporting dynamic with their department leader. At the same time, every staff leader (and their family, where applicable) identifies with a specific Southridge location. Thus, they simultaneously belong to a location-specific team which includes members from all departments. This is their "dotted-line" reporting dynamic. In our context, we chose the solid line reporting to be departmental, as opposed to location-specific, because our shared mission of fostering a lifestyle of full devotion is our highest value as a church, more so than the current specifics of the location where that mission plays out.

In the solid-line reporting dynamic, people belong to their ministry team. They have direct and ongoing supervisory support from their leader. It's in this context where they develop their performance plans and receive their annual performance evaluation. The dotted-line reporting dynamic occurs less frequently; location-specific teams seek to meet every month or two. While also evaluating the effectiveness of the primary programs in their specific location, the focus of the location-specific team, led by the location pastor, is to add value to the personal touch of pastoral care and support. Helping incorporate new people, caring for existing people, engaging idle people, and following up with people who would potentially fall through the cracks, the location-specific team allows larger church leaders to behave like smaller church leaders too.

On top of both of these work dynamics, though, is a leader's (and their household's) personal identity with a location and its specific Anchor Cause. In addition to solid line reporting as departments and dotted line reporting as location teams we deliberately encourage personal engagement in the Anchor Cause of their location. Oftentimes, then, the Anchor Cause Director of that particular location also has a leadership role in the lives of our ministry leaders, ensuring they're actively mobilized for compassion and justice. Maybe this only requires temporary attention for a time but given the church's default to gathering and occasionally grouping, extra deliberacy to engage every leader at Southridge in the Action aspect of the lifestyle of full devotion is key to us leading (and living) as a missional church.

The Ministry of Management

That thought actually leads to another critical aspect to our approach to structure: how to organize your people for maximum ministry effectiveness. Over the years, we've learned two critical lessons to make the most of our local church's ministry. For starters, we've learned to mobilize the *lifestyle before the ministry*. What that means is, as someone is engaging with your church, regardless of whichever primary program serves as the "front door" to your community for them (weekend services, Life Groups, Anchor Causes, or Family Ministry), our goal, and discipleship plan, is to activate them across the primary programs as full participants before they become contributors to one or more of those areas of ministry. Oftentimes in churches—again, especially in attractional-model structures—a weekend service attender will "engage" by serving in a first impressions ministry before and/or after the service, or they'll "give back" by serving in the children's ministry on Sunday mornings. This sense of input-output leaves many churchgoers feeling complete but misses out on the comprehensive discipleship of the "lecture-seminar-co-op" triumvirate of a three-dimensional ministry model. In our context, we'd much rather see someone from our weekend service grow as a fully orbed participant in Jesus' way of life before becoming part of the ministry leadership that drives our weekend service. Busy people (especially those with limited devotion) only have so much space in their lives for ministry activity, so we'd rather grow fully orbed followers than partially orbed leaders.

Once someone does engage on the leadership side of the equation, the other critical aspect of attention we've discovered is the gift mix and leadership style of the *kind of impact* someone wants to make. In summary, some are *doers*; they love to affect people directly, in a hands-on fashion. Some are *leaders*; they love to mobilize doers and multiply their impact. And some are *facilitators*; they love to enable leaders to mobilize doers and, in that way, further multiply their impact, albeit indirectly. The more someone biases towards a facilitator, the more comfortable they need to be with having only a vicarious impact on church participants, as opposed to the direct life-on-life impact of a ministry doer.

This matters—big time—for two reasons. First, from the theological perspective, the work of the church is intended by God to be done by the people of the church. Theologians call it the priesthood of *all* believers, because every single body part in the body of Christ is necessary for Christ to fully be at work through the church in the world today. From a theological perspective, the role of a church leader is not to do the work of the church, but rather to equip the doers of the work of the church—like Paul describes in Ephesians 4:11–13: *"Christ himself gave the apostles, the prophets, the evangelists, the pastors and teachers, to equip his people for works of service, so that the body of Christ may be built up until we all reach unity in the faith and in the knowledge of the Son of God and become mature, attaining to the whole measure of the fullness of Christ."* In theory (or theology), it's critical to ensure that doer-types are aligned with doer work and equipper-types are deployed in equipper roles.

At the end of the day though, it matters even more in practice. Not only does it frustrate doers to be positioned in indirect-impact roles, it also frustrates the other doers in direct-impact roles that their role is supposed to equip. Often it seems that the best doers become leaders. And in churches like ours, too many times we've appointed the best leaders as facilitators (leaders who lead leaders). What we've had to embrace is that there's a distinct ministry in addition to providing ministry and providing leadership. We call it: *providing management*. And we actually refer to this more senior-leadership level as the Ministry of Management, intending to redeem a word that feels corporate and spiritless.

The truth, though, is that a ministry so complicated as to seek to foster a lifestyle of full devotion in three dimensions, plus in age-appropriate ways, with an operations support system, in multiple locations, where each site is focused on and defined by its own unique Anchor Cause, requires significant organizational support from its most senior leaders. While they all need servant's hearts and Christ's character to shine through them, a ministry seeking to deliver these outcomes can't have its most senior leaders be primarily doers. To thrive, it can't even have leaders who still like or need to feel the direct impact of their ministry on people. This most senior layer of leadership requires facilitators—those with a bias to indirect, vicarious impact through layers of leaders and doers—in order to provide the vision, organization, communication, problem-solving, and conflict-resolution kinds of supports that a ministry of doers mobilized by leaders requires. Simply put: value the Ministry of Management, so the entire puzzle of people and leaders can be put together most effectively.

At the end of the day, that's actually the value of good organizational structure: that the complex puzzle—or system—of your local part of the body of Christ can be put together as well as possible. Not every church looks like ours or requires the same structure as ours. But every church does require a leadership structure that equips the people to do the ministry, according to their unique gifts. And at the very end of the day, good organizational structure doesn't exist for the sake of good organizational structure. It exists for the sake of love. Remember: the wineskin is the system and structure. The wine is the incarnational life and love of Jesus Christ. But consider the New Living Translation of Paul's description of Jesus in Ephesians 4:16—*"Jesus makes the whole body fit together perfectly. As each part does its own special work, it helps the other parts grow, so that the whole body is healthy and growing and full of love."* That's why systems and structure matter, because love matters most!

10

Becoming a Missional Church

How DOES A LOCAL church operationalize compassion and justice ministry? Especially if your church biases towards disproportionately focusing on its gatherings (maybe even in ways that unconsciously or unintentionally cater to peoples' consumerism), what is the process for transforming your ministry? If your church, and even its sites (in a multi-site dynamic), were to be defined less by the place and time you gather, and more by the difference it made in their surrounding society, where would you start in the process of building towards that end? How, practically, do you transition from a primarily attractional to a predominantly missional church?

Having now launched and grown three distinct Anchor Causes at three separate locations and grown our ministry's financial "pie" allocation of local and global compassion and justice from zero to now over 70 percent of all the money we spend, we've noticed a pattern that has become our guiding process for operationalizing compassion and justice. Starting chronologically, this chapter will walk through the key stages of development that every single Anchor Cause has had to navigate, while at the same time describing the customization that each Southridge location has had to be creative in meeting the unique needs in their respective communities.

The 4-P Process

It was in St. Catharines where we were originally haunted by our inability to answer the question, "If your church suddenly disappeared, would anyone

75

in the surrounding society even notice?" In response to this question, our first step was to move. The relocation of our church from a rural agrarian setting to a mile from the downtown core of our city was critical to establishing a presence of compassion and justice. Similar to Jesus' Great Commission to, *"Go and make disciples . . ."* the initiative to go to where the needs are, instead of expecting those in need to come to you, has become integral to our church's capacity to incarnate the life and love of Jesus in our community. So, in this first case, our first step was to establish *proximity* to the very people we intended to serve.

As we moved into the city, though, our first instinct wasn't to immediately launch ministry. To the contrary, our default assumption, which proved powerful in this process, was to believe that God was already at work in this place (as opposed to arrogantly assuming we'd be the only game in town), and we began by first discovering where and how God was already working in order to come alongside him to a greater degree. In his book *Experiencing God*, Henry Blackaby encourages people to stop asking God to bless what they're doing and instead discern what God's already blessing and start doing it. In this spirit, then, our first move as city-dwellers was simply to activate our peoples' spiritual muscles of compassion and justice by encouraging them to be involved with some ministries that we *partnered* with.

As I described earlier in Chapter 5, one of those key partnerships was with an inter-church ministry to the homeless called Out of the Cold. We served as the Sunday night site for the homeless of St. Catharines from November 1 to March 31 each winter for two years, until the mayor of the city of St. Catharines approached us and asked if we'd continue to open our facility space to feed and house homeless people, full-time, throughout the months when Out of the Cold wasn't in operation. Had we not partnered with Out of the Cold, we would have had no idea that the void of sheltering people during the summer even existed and would have never realized our church's capacity to meet that need with our facility and people. So, in response to discovering this gap in the support system of what God was already doing—a gap we could only discover through partnership—we were able to be intelligent about how to launch our own core *program* that could come alongside the existing supports for the homeless of St. Catharines, to complement and supplement the ministry that was already happening instead of competing against it.

From there, though, we knew that our intention for opening a homeless shelter was not limited to offering emergency shelter. By this time, we'd seen the values (again, described in more detail in Chapter 5) of extending Christ's love, cultivating experiential discipleship, and creating new evangelistic front doors that fostering relationships of mutuality with the homeless provided. And as we discovered that "friendship makes the difference," we saw the hostel ministry (the "three hots and a cot" that are core to an emergency shelter) as merely the starting point. In short, we understood that this core program would ultimately serve as a launchpad for these transformational relationships to form. So, we began to develop social extensions of the shelter—programs like sports nights, arts club, games evenings, summer barbeque nights, retreats, Christmas parties, and many more—in order to ensure that this core program functioned in a way that *promoted the lifestyle* of full devotion it was intended by God and our church leadership to do.

By reflecting on our experience of launching our ministry to the homeless in St. Catharines, we noticed this four-stage process of: establishing proximity, developing partnerships, launching core programs, and ensuring they promote lifestyle. So, when we started to imagine becoming a multi-site church and people immediately asked our leadership what the "shelter-equivalent" would be in these new sites, we used these reflections to generate a roadmap for the establishment of future Anchor Causes.

Different Need, Same Process

When we launched a Southridge location in Welland (about a twenty-minute drive south of St. Catharines), we experimented with these same four steps. Obviously, the act of launching the location itself was the first step, motivating a core of our existing folks who lived in that part of Niagara. Becoming a Southridge location in this part of Niagara represented our desire for the Southridge members who were residents of this community to be proximal to the needs of their society. Again, we weren't expecting the needs to come to us. By launching the site, we were coming to them.

And again, assuming that God was already at work in the Welland area, we looked to establish some preliminary partnerships to get involved in what God was doing to activate the spiritual muscles of compassion and justice in our people. We narrowed our options down to the three most reputable and effective partnerships available to us, all with an eye on serving low-income families, particularly sole-support parents and children, which was identified by survey data and political leaders as the greatest need in the community at the time. Our people began to involve themselves in these partner ministries that served to support these at-risk families, making investments in parents and establishing relationships with kids.

In this case, this stage of the process actually lasted much longer than in St. Catharines because for years we gathered on weekends in rented facilities. (We were known locally as "the church that comes from St. Catharines on weekends.") What we had come to appreciate was that for our church to have a missional presence in a community, that could function as a "playground" for developing transformational relationships, we required a home-base facility for ourselves. Eventually we were able to locate and purchase a suitable facility where our own core programs could be launched. As God would have it, the physical location he provided happened to border on one of the neighborhoods that we served through our most key partnership, enabling us to naturally complement and supplement what these amazing ministries were already doing.

In Welland, the most obvious need of many of our low-income families is affordable housing, and we've already begun discussions with local government officials and construction experts to determine whether some of our location's five acres of property ought to be leveraged for this purpose. But in absence of providing direct relief to that core need, we discovered that one of the greatest needs that existed was with food security. So, in our new facility we developed a couple core programs around food support. One, called Harvest Kitchen, functions simply as a community meal, where every Friday night members of the broader community and members of our church enjoy a meal at mixed tables with one another. The second core program, called Collective Kitchen, functions as a meal-preparation program where clients and church members make meals together throughout a full day, where participants can leave with twenty-five freezer meals for their family for just $25.

I'm sure you can see how, in both of these cases, these programs are conducive to promoting the lifestyle of full devotion, especially as it relates to Action, because of how relationship-stimulating they are. Like the shelter in St. Catharines, the core programs of our Anchor Cause in Welland serve as launchpads for relationships to spark. And it's through the establishment of these otherwise unlikely friendships that a variety of other practical needs get met in families, our people experience spiritual "aha" moments, and others can join in directly to living out the life and love of Jesus as a desirable first step of engagement in our church. While addressing a completely different need, the 4-P process played out similarly in our Welland Anchor Cause.

Be Creative Inside the Box!

When we launched our Vineland Location, then (about a twenty-minute drive west of St. Catharines), we were pretty committed to establishing our Anchor Cause and core programs in this way. Rather than feeling rigid or stifling though, the guidance provided through this sequential framework actually allowed our creativity and innovation to flow. I once heard that Walt Disney used to say that "To be creative, you needed to think *inside* the box." This has become our experience when it comes to launching our Anchor Causes.

Once again, relocating local families from our Southridge core in St. Catharines to our new Vineland location represented the "us-coming-to-them" step of establishing proximity. Church members were eager to become the hands and feet of Jesus in their home neighborhood. In this part of Niagara, full of fruit farms, the greatest marginalization tended to be experienced by seasonal Caribbean farm workers. Sensing that reciprocal friendship could once again make the difference, we established partnerships with a couple of key ministries and support services that had served seasonal migrant farm workers for years.

When we, once again, discovered some gaps in support for this community, that we as a local church could fill, we launched into the backbone of our core programming through a Life Group "adopt-a-farm" program. Each Vineland Life Group was assigned the migrant workers of an area farm and was tasked with regularly socializing with, supporting, and surprising their guys. Immediately, friendships began to form. To stimulate that further, we offered Sunday evening larger-group social nights at our Vineland Location throughout the summer months. Jerk chicken barbeques, cricket matches, and domino tournaments highlighted the activities of these summer evenings, where workers from a variety of farms could interact with each other and the families of our church in fun and relaxed ways.

Through the initial establishment of these relationships, though, we quickly began to see a deficiency in these workers' access to reasonable health care. If someone had medical issues, they either had to take time off work to see a doctor (something they could hardly afford, and their employers weren't always fond of) or they remained faithful at work and left their medical issues unaddressed. So, again in partnership with a local agency, we renovated two basement rooms of our Vineland Location to house fully functioning medical clinics. During each Sunday evening social we offered free, after-hours medical support, fully staffed by Southridge doctors and nurses. The combination of social nights and medical support became the core expression of our Anchor Cause programming, building off our Life Group adopt-a-farm starting point.

Since then, we've been able to promote the lifestyle of Action through worker's welcome concerts, social outings to Niagara Falls, or area sporting events, and an end-of-season harvest celebration. As well, we send a team of Southridge members to Jamaica each winter for a visit (not to be confused with a mission trip; see Chapter 11 for more thinking on our approach to Global Missions). For many of our Vineland Location members, mornings like Christmas Day are highlighted by phone calls or FaceTime calls with their Caribbean friends. And as we collect worker's welcome kits at Christmas, or invite others into the larger-group activities, these relationships provide an easy invite to friends of our Vineland members from outside the church to join in as well. Once again, by following this very simple process along a unique path for this location, we've been able to enjoy the "friendship that makes the difference" through our Anchor Cause in Vineland.

Grow by Focusing on Need

The beautiful part of this story is that none of our location's Anchor Causes are static; they continue to evolve and develop. The key has been to not only start with a societal need, but to continue to refine and expand on our capacity to more effectively serve that need. The heart to serve even better drives the ministry's growth.

One fascinating example of this was when one of our leaders started to wonder how we could better support our homeless shelter residents and former residents with life skills and job training. Teaming up with kitchen staff from our shelter, they started experimenting with the process of jam-making as a way to provide work experience and develop marketable skills to residents and former residents. As this idea evolved, a leader from our Vineland Anchor Cause started reaching out to area fruit farmers (from the farms where our Life Groups had adopted their workers) and they began donating their fruit—not leftovers, but first-rate fruit—to this fledgling initiative.

After receiving a charitable grant to industrialize the kitchen in our Vineland Location (the only kitchen in our Southridge Locations that wasn't already regularly being used for Anchor Cause activity), we launched a social enterprise where jam, made by people impacted by homelessness, to provide life development and skill training, was sold in farmer's markets, boutique shops, and grocery stores, so the proceeds of the jam sales could be reinvested in more supports for our homeless shelter. Today, southridgejam.com provides "good jam, with a great story" and has become the free gift we provide for new attendees of our weekend gatherings. It is yet another way to not just foster "friendship that makes the difference," but also to help change the brand of how the church is perceived in the surrounding community, and to offer a new front door for those who are seeking faith.

The point here is this: through following the basic stages of this Anchor Cause development process, you can begin to operationalize compassion and justice ministry in your local church. With a focus on addressing societal needs, a humble and collaborative posture, and a discerning spirit, you can allow God to guide you uniquely to meet specific needs in your society in noticeable ways. And by organizing your community around meeting those needs in ways that can mobilize the masses (an Anchor Cause core program has to be able to involve everybody), you can start cultivating the kinds of launchpads where "friendship makes the difference" in your local church too.

I'm excited to see where God might lead our church to launch future Anchor Causes. And I'm excited to see how he'll mature our faith and grow us beyond merely expressing compassion to become legitimate advocates for justice among the underprivileged in our society. Most of all, though, I'm thrilled to see where God might lead you to launch one in your part of the world and how he'll grow you and your people through it. And I'm thrilled to see how an increased commitment to operationalizing compassion and justice ministry, instead of continuing to primarily or exclusively focus on enhancing our gatherings, can help foster a lifestyle of full devotion to Jesus across your community and help change the impression people have of the Christian church in your part of the world. They'll know we are Christians by our love. May your church's good deeds create goodwill that leads people to the good news of Jesus like never before!

11

Global Missions

FOR YEARS, I NEVER felt settled in my spirit when it came to how our church extended compassion and justice globally. I could never put a finger on why. I just knew that something was off and needed to be done differently. Historically, our church had engaged in what felt like a token engagement: two budget line items representing about 1 percent of our total budget that were designated as goals to reach (not even amounts we were necessarily committed to) to support a couple of denominationally affiliated global mission organizations. A few years into our ministry, we began to explore some more direct opportunities, creating experiences where our people could be personally involved in mission work, sending people on trips to paint orphanages or build schools. And while it seemed to be more direct, in my spirit it didn't seem to necessarily be any more effective, and I couldn't help but wonder whether it was making a positive impact at all.

Eventually, our action pastor at the time took a deep dive into researching models and approaches for global mission. Along with a subcommittee of experienced and wise church members, he investigated mission agencies, consulted with local churches from around the world, and researched available resources on the topic. All told, we invested four years into the discernment process of how best to move forward as a local church seeking to foster a lifestyle of full devotion to Jesus from the perspective of global compassion and justice. To us, it was incredible how much God was able to distill and clarify once we slowed down long enough to pay attention and consider the most basic questions of how he wanted to work among us, and what was stopping us from allowing him to do so. This chapter seeks to walk you through our journey, and hopefully save you some of the four years of that investment.

What's Wrong with This Picture?

The first thing our deep dive into global missions helped us clarify was what was so dissatisfying about our previous approaches. We knew we weren't having the impact a local church ultimately was intended by God to have in this regard, we just couldn't articulate why. Upon reflection and analysis, we realized that we were mixing up and confusing our values, in ways that crossed purposes and resulted in ineffective ministry.

For example, when we stopped and reflected on the mission trips we had designed, we were able to face the reality that nothing we were sending our people to other countries to do couldn't be done by people from those countries themselves. Out of a desire to activate our people, we were wasting tens of thousands of travel dollars and robbing local people of the opportunity to make a difference in their own world. At the same time, to simply toss money at a mission agency felt impersonal; out of sight, out of mind. It often felt unaccountable too, where in many cases the mission agency simply supported people in fuller-time ways to do the very same thing we tried to do with our own people: perform tasks in a developing country that locals could do themselves.

We wondered whether sending certain people or families to serve as global missionaries was the answer—a little more personal, and perhaps a little more specialized—until we started to track their journeys. Take a couple, for example, who served overseas for a multi-year period. Raising their own support, they managed to collect the hundreds of thousands of dollars required to send and fund their family's multi-year mission. But year one was primarily devoted to cultural acclimatization and training; aside from homeschooling their own children, the couple studied the native language and customs in order to adapt. Year two was a little more active, although a large portion of the couple's time was still required for the homeschooling of their children. At this point, though, they were able to start involving themselves directly in the mission project they'd been sent for. Unfortunately, by year three, some relational tensions emerged, and they shifted their focus to serving in a local orphanage instead of the originally intended mission project. And after three years, they felt their calling change and headed home.

I realize this can become very uncomfortable to address, but as a leadership we had to stare examples like this in the face and ask: what just happened? People from our community essentially paid a family to do ministry, full-time, in a setting they were unfamiliar with, without identifying in advance any specific skills that equipped them for that particular ministry. We essentially "hired" two adults that, in our church, we would have never hired for full-time ministry, but somehow it felt like those stewardship values didn't apply once you left the country. And after three years, they returned with wonderful family memories and some homeschooled children, but—here's the really uncomfortable part—virtually nothing to show for the investment made in them. While certainly not every foreign missionary's story is like this one, we felt the obligation to revisit outcomes like these, which seem to occur too often.

What Did We Really Want?

At some point, we had to face the reality Jesus taught his disciples to appreciate in Luke 19, where all of us have been entrusted with kingdom resources and all of us are expected to yield a return on the investment of those resources. To faithfully steward the resources God has entrusted to you receives the *"well done, my good and faithful servant!"* And yet the king refers to the servant who squandered the resources with which he was entrusted as wicked. We had to appreciate that, both personally and as a church, there was a stewardship obligation where we were accountable to God and each other to optimize the kingdom return on the resources we invested globally, not just locally. Our responsibility as a local church leadership was to *maximize stewardship* of our church's resources when it came to extending global compassion and justice.

At the same time, it was more than math. We weren't just referring to finances. The reason we tried personal approaches, rather than merely donating funds to a global mission agency, was that we felt we needed a more personal touch. After more reflection and analysis, what we were able to clarify was that, since fostering a lifestyle of full devotion to Jesus was our church's overall objective, and because Jesus intended his followers to spread his life and love *". . . to the ends of the earth"* by the power of his Holy Spirit, we were actually responsible to form every single Christ follower in our care into a more *global* missionary. We weren't allowed to view this as merely financial. We were also responsible to *maximize discipleship* of our people from a global compassion and justice perspective as well; to turn everyone into missionaries.

As simple as this may seem in hindsight (and may be all along to you and your church), that was the "aha"-level clarity we needed, that as a leadership we had two responsibilities when it came to our local church extending global compassion and justice. To maximize our church's impact, we needed to maximize our stewardship and maximize our discipleship. That's what we want our global missions' efforts to do: make the greatest difference in the world that we can with the resources God entrusts to us *and* to activate as many missionaries as we can within our church. Those two values helped us understand what felt unsettled in some of our previous experiences and, more importantly, what we were shooting for in establishing an operationalized global compassion and justice presence as a local church.

Partnering with Compassion

The next question, though, was: what do we do with this newfound clarity? We still weren't experts on much of this, so where could we turn to start achieving these two objectives? Through our four-year investigative process, one of the agencies we consulted with was Compassion International—and particularly their national affiliate here, Compassion Canada. While we appreciated (and still do!) many of the other global mission agencies we consulted and hold their international relief and development work in high regard, what struck us about Compassion was that they valued these same two objectives. They desired to make the greatest difference globally, but also desired to activate as many people as possible into becoming personal global missionaries. In addition, their whole philosophy of ministry is centred around the ministry of the *local church*, that the local church is not only responsible for caring for the condition of the brokenness in their part of the world, but that within it, there is the capacity to provide the most ongoing and holistic comprehensive support to those in need. So, we began to create a partnership with Compassion Canada where these values could be lived out in growing ways.

We started by focusing on maximizing discipleship, where Compassion representatives partnered with us to overhaul our mobilization approach. Together, we developed a curriculum called a Global Action Plan (GAP), which takes our members through lessons and experiences to awaken them to the realities of global poverty, of Western privilege, and of God's intent for Christ followers to share in the responsibility to care for the condition of the brokenness of the world. Members discover how to contribute to alleviating issues of global poverty and injustice without ever necessarily needing to get on an airplane as they develop a growing awareness of injustice surrounding issues such as shopping, environmentalism, racism, and marginalization. Supported by Compassion Canada staff and resources, we've been able to take hundreds of our core people through the experience of our GAP.

In turn, we've been able to maximize the stewardship of our church's resources by partnering with Compassion in their Survival initiatives. Functioning like Anchor Causes in local churches around the world, these initiatives focus on new mothers and their babies from pregnancy through the first year of their lives. Aside from spiritual support, they receive practical equipping on parenting, ongoing medical support, dietary assistance, and other aspects of childhood development, in order to holistically wrap the arms of Jesus around these young mothers. The beauty is, because locals are directly caring for locals, supported through the expertise and resources of Compassion, these local churches can establish long-term relationships with people in their own community where (just like at Southridge) friendship makes the difference." And from an economic perspective, the cost to invest in resourcing a single Survival program that serves dozens of moms and babies is a small fraction of the cost of sending a single missionary overseas. Investing in the work of overseas local churches increases the stewardship of our local church.

The best part of this partnership, though, isn't the way Compassion has helped us maximize discipleship or the way we've invested in their Survival programs to maximize stewardship. It's the way we've been able to maximize relationships. What ties both of these initiatives together is Compassion's Child Development Sponsorship Program (CDSP). On the one hand, encouraging each GAP graduate to sponsor a child allows them to establish a direct relationship with one family globally and experientially learn about global compassion and justice. On the other hand, each of the Survival programs we sponsor through Compassion now provide their graduates, babies who as young children now enter the CDSP, for our people to directly sponsor. So, our collective financial giving supports babies who become sponsor children, which sets the stage for discipleship through personal sponsorship. And through the long-term, ongoing strengthening of that sponsorship relationship—through prayer, letter-writing, special supplementary gifts (for birthdays, Christmas, etc.), and even sponsor visits facilitated by Compassion—every one of our growing global missionaries can personally make a difference as part of a church that's collectively making a difference in ways that maximize stewardship and discipleship through relationship.

Our Global Anchor Cause

Today, we now identify Child Survival as our church's Global Anchor Cause. In addition to our local Anchor Causes that define each particular Southridge location, our Global Anchor Cause unites our whole church with this global perspective and engagement. Currently, we sponsor seven Compassion Survival programs, at least one in every continent, and these program graduates become the children our members are encouraged to sponsor. As well, about one-third of our church population has been activated to sponsor a child through Compassion, and through initiatives like our annual "Hope Lives" weekend message series and our location café artwork, our people are regularly reminded of the power that sponsorship provides for experiencing reciprocally transformative relationship.

We are not only seeing growing impact through the local churches around the world that we partner with through our Compassion-sponsored Survival programs. We're seeing the growing impact on our own people through their child sponsorships and beyond. In some cases, the growing awareness of global issues has triggered greater engagement in issues of poverty and marginalization locally as well, even beyond the scope of our locations' Anchor Causes. In others, it's inspired people to activate themselves directly into global mission issues, contributing to disaster relief and international development. Once, when we walked our people through an experience with the "Global Rich List," some residents of our homeless shelter awakened to their relative wealth on a global scale and began to raise funds from among their fellow residents' daily allowances to support entrepreneurs in the developing world. These days, our homeless shelter residents have raised thousands of dollars for Kiva loans, a beautiful picture of disciples becoming missionaries!

From the perspective of a local church pastor, the beauty in all of this is that now I don't feel like our church is limited to paying for a few select people in our community to have global impact. Through our partnership with Compassion, we're investing in all of our people growing our global impact, while being transformed in the process, and also providing a missing piece of the puzzle for local churches around the world to rally around specific needs in their community. We know our approach to global missions isn't perfect, and we're constantly ideating about where God may seek to grow it in the future. But after years of frustration and confusion, we're starting to see God maximize our stewardship and maximize our discipleship through maximizing relationships, particularly through our partnership with Compassion Canada.

This hasn't just been something I've observed. It's something my family and I have had the chance to personally experience. Flowing out of some early initiatives that encouraged child sponsorship, our family began sponsoring a boy in Guatemala. Early on my wife planned a visit to meet him and his family, and for the past decade one of our family's annual vacations has been to Guatemala for a sponsor family visit. After a few years we were also able to sponsor his younger sister as well, so our relationship with this family has only strengthened. In recent months, we were able to travel to Guatemala to host our sponsor daughter's quinceanera, her coming-of-age party celebrating her fifteenth birthday. Not only has God strengthened our global perspective through this relationship, but as he's seared our hearts together as an extended family, we've experienced his work in all of us in miraculous ways.

By seeking to maximize discipleship and maximize stewardship, through the crucible of maximizing relationship, your local church can grow in its global impact. You can begin seeing and celebrating the ways God develops global missionaries of all of your people, not just a random, select few. And you can experience stories of God's transforming work in up-close-and-personal ways even though you're halfway across the globe. As a local church leader, you can become settled in your spirit as your church extends compassion and justice globally in ways worth celebrating.

12

Generational Transfer of Leadership

OUR CHURCH WAS FOUNDED in 1980 by a group of young families who wanted to do church differently, specifically in ways that would engage their kids. Their goal was to do ministry in a way that their kids would grow up knowing, loving, and serving Jesus. In those early years, the ministry of our church was defined by numerous activities for kids: a "children's feature" as part of each weekend service, midweek ministry, and children's choirs, as well as other special events, family retreats, and socials. With this focus on their kids, the hope was to raise up the next generation of Jesus followers.

Fast-forward to the mid-1990s, when our founding pastor sought to retire. As I understand it, the church had struggled to find a replacement, striking out with their search committee and recruitment process. In a meeting of the church's board, though, someone observed that among the board members who owned their own small businesses, they were each starting the process of handing those businesses over to their kids. If "Option A" in their private lives was to hand their family businesses over to their kids, they wondered, why couldn't "Option A" as a church be to hand its leadership over to its next generation as well? In a sense, this epiphany brought the founding value of investing in the next generation full circle and into its legitimate fulfillment.

That led the board to appoint one younger leader named Chris Fowler as an apprentice pastor. Soon enough though, the apprentice was envisioning the founding pastor, who quickly felt ready, willing, and able to retire (and to our joy, he remains an active participant in our church even today!).

Coming from a music and worship background, Chris soon felt himself needing support in preaching and teaching, so on September 1, 1997, both Michael Krause (who had been part of the church since its inception) and me (whose family started at the church in 1983, when I was only ten years old) were brought on board to help Chris lead the church, particularly by providing teaching. The rest, you could say, is history!

Along that journey (while far from perfect), I observed some critical dynamics that enabled this process (which we've formally referred to as the generational transfer of leadership) to work effectively. And for any local church leader wrestling with succession issues or looking to mobilize the next generation into its church leadership, there were three critical questions our church leaders had to face and deal with effectively. For clarity's sake, as I describe these dynamics, I'll refer to the two generations as "First Generation" and "Second Generation." Words matter, and I find that referring to people as "older" or "younger" for whatever reason carries with it the various pieces of cultural baggage, prejudice, and disrespect. So, I'll use these more neutral terms to try to foster a mutuality of honor right from the get-go.

The "Why?" Question

The first thing that was done well, right from the very beginning, was the shared clarity about this process. Our First-Generation church leaders were clear from the outset that this was a formal process and committed for the long haul to hand the "family business" of our church over to its kids. It wasn't done in secret or through backroom negotiations. This was a repeatedly publicly stated intent by our leadership that invited the rest of our church into the journey of making this a reality.

Simply put: our existing church leaders embraced and shared God's vision for generational transfer. As described in places like Psalm 79:13, God has intended for there to be continuity among the people of his family: *"Then we your people, the sheep of your pasture, will praise you forever; from generation to generation we will proclaim your praise."* Our leaders inspired our people to embrace the biblical dynamic of a "from generation to generation" church. And as the years progressed, they continually anchored their public conversations in this fundamental reason for why we were doing this.

At the same time, our Second-Generation leaders embraced this dynamic too. We understood that we weren't being invited into roles or jobs, but actually a long-term process of transitioning into our church's leadership. From the very beginning of our ministry life, people like Chris, Michael, and me framed our sense of calling and commitment around a "forty-year vision." At one point, Chris actually had to withdraw for a period of time for health reasons, and the First-Generation leadership immediately looked to Michael and me and asked, "Are you still in?" That all of us from both generations were committed to the long-haul nature of fulfilling this vision proved essential to its success. Trying to start by framing it as a "short-term experiment" would have never worked.

For First-Generation leaders reading this: are you willing to embrace God's vision for generational transfer by passing the leadership of your church to the next generation? And what are you doing to create those opportunities today, right now, for those emerging leaders in your community? And for Second-Generation leaders: will you work together with the existing leaders of your church in order to facilitate the process of handing over this spiritual family business? And what are you doing today, right now, to step into those opportunities and to discern whether God is inviting you to give your one and only life to being the next generation of the church? In a dynamic like this, it certainly does take "two to tango," and both generations need to fully embrace the vision of God to see the from-generation-to-generation continuity of leadership among the people of his spiritual family.

The "What?" Question

Aside from that willingness, though, what our church's leaders did well was deliver on the requisite aspects of what the process of generational transfer requires. While it takes a long-term commitment, there are some specific requirements that must be fulfilled in order for generational transfer to stick. It doesn't "just happen" over time. It requires some specific, concrete commitments in order to realize it.

The basis for these commitments is rooted in how biblical church leadership works. In a passage like 1 Peter 5, for example, we see Peter instructing leaders this way: *"To the elders among you, I appeal as a fellow elder and a witness of Christ's sufferings who also will share in the glory to be revealed: Be shepherds of God's flock that is under your care, serving as overseers."* In this encouragement, Peter uses two very disparate terms to describe the role of church leaders. One is a "shepherd," which, in his context, was a very down-and-dirty role of the responsibility to lead the community. The other was an "overseer," which, to the contrary, seemed to emphasize the high esteem and authority of this leadership. What's critical to note is that both of these terms are used together; that, in God's economy, healthy leadership is the *linking of authority and responsibility* together.

What that means, at a technical level, is that the transfer of leadership from one generation to another is actually the reassignment of *both* authority *and* responsibility, from one group who holds both in a primary way to a second group who holds neither but over time embraces both. To simplify this, I'd draw out the process this way:

$$AR + ar \rightarrow ar + AR$$

In this simple equation, the First Generation has transferred the primary authority and responsibility of leadership over to the Second Generation. This is what the process of generational transfer requires because healthy leadership is the linkage of both authority and responsibility together.

Can you see, though, how this process can break down? On the one hand, First Generation leaders can be eager for the next generation to be involved and help carry the load but can still desire to retain control. This skews the diagram this way:

$$AR + ar \rightarrow Ar + aR$$

In this case, the Second Generation has been given responsibility but lacks the authority and influence that ought to go with it. They may be fresh horsepower in the church, but they're not even remotely the leaders of the church quite yet.

The same is true when the Second Generation desires to implement all their new ideas and methods for the church, but still expects the first generation to pay for it or continue doing all the dirty work that's less appealing. Then things skew this way:

$$AR + ar \rightarrow aR + Ar$$

In this case, the Second Generation will easily embrace having influence and authority but not be fully prepared to bear the full responsibility of leading a spiritual family. (As John Maxwell has said, "Too often people want to do what I do without having done what I've done.") In this case, the

First Generation is being treated as the primary resourcing and horsepower to fuel and drive a next generation's vision and new ideas.

In our case, both generations of leadership embraced their unique obligations for making this process work in a healthy way. Our First-Generation leaders allowed those of us emerging leaders to share in and have influence in the most primary influential environments, allowing our voices in their boardroom and giving us the platform of the pulpit. We weren't just being asked to pick up the slack of whatever they no longer wanted to do. Similarly, our Second-Generation leaders embraced the full responsibility of being allowed these opportunities for influence, specifically when it came to shepherding people (especially First-Generation people) through crises, navigating difficult or delicate conversations, or facing financial and fundraising challenges. We weren't just looking to *have* a voice, but to *become* a voice through the responsibility we bore for the health and future of our community.

In this way, do you understand what the process of generational transfer actually requires—specifically for each unique generation? First-Generation leaders: do you recognize that your bias will be to resist giving away authority? Will you allow the next generation to have primary influence in the future of your church? And Second-Generation leaders: do you appreciate that your bias will be to resist assuming the full responsibility? Will you embrace all of what it takes, not just the parts you're personally passionate about, to comprehensively spiritually parent a community of faith? If everyone can keep the dynamics of authority and responsibility in church leadership linked together, the process of generational transfer can transition leadership in a healthy way.

The "How?" Question

The final piece we found critical to an effective process of generational transfer involved the perspective we collectively shared about how things would look in the future. It goes without saying that different generations bring different perspectives, but it's essential to say out loud that the process of generational transfer is, over time, the journey towards the future and away from the past. Mutually embracing how the church will look and work in the future, and predominantly that it will look and work *differently* than it does today, is a critical component to the process.

In Philippians 3:13, the apostle Paul describes this kind of perspective this way: *"I focus on this one thing: forgetting the past and looking forward to what lies ahead."* A life of faith, and particularly a life of leadership in a community of faith, is ultimately future-oriented, not primarily past-preserving. For a long-term generational transfer process to work effectively, everyone has to share that bias for a future orientation together. While respecting the history and tradition of the community, you have to create the future together as opposed to simply protecting the past.

Of course, this plays out differently for each generation. First Generation leaders need to embrace the new ideas, and particularly, the new methods, that a next generation of leaders bring. As Jesus taught, *"New wine must be stored in new wineskins"* and if First Generation leaders expect the next generation to simply add fresh energy to their ways of doing church, they'll never engage them for the long-haul. By contrast, Second Generation leaders must bring a respect for their past to their envisioning and implementing of their ideas and methods for the future, and consider the wisdom of their previous generation's leadership experience. Read through 1 Kings chapter 12 again, the story of Solomon's son Rehoboam, and watch how a generational transfer breaks down. Because *"Rehoboam rejected the advice the elders gave him and (only) consulted the young men who had grown up with him and were serving him,"* the family of God was permanently fractured.

There are serious consequences to communities of faith when we fail to reciprocally honor one another with a view to the future. First Generation leaders: are you actively encouraging the new ideas and methods of the next generation, or are you expecting these new-wine leaders to propagate the old wineskins of how you prefer church to be done? Are you truly future-oriented or do you consistently bias towards preserving and protecting the past? Likewise, are you Second-Generation leaders respecting the input and advice of the existing leadership of your church, even actively seeking out their wisdom and experience? While orienting to the future, are you respectful of the past and seeking to retain ways in which God has worked effectively? This reciprocal relationship of mutual honor—at a daily, change-by-change level—can be the biggest deal-breaker to a healthy process of generational transfer.

I would encourage you to collect groups of key leadership in your church from both generations to process these three foundational questions together. In imagining a succession or transfer of leadership from one generation to the next, are you clear on *why* you'd even bother launching into such a challenging journey? Do you really want to be a from-generation-to-generation community of faith? More importantly, are you clear on *what* the process of healthy generational transfer requires, linking authority and responsibility together? And will you each do your part to allow this healthy transition, letting go of your need for control (First Generation) and stepping up to embrace the full responsibility (Second Generation) of spiritually parenting God's family? Most critical of all, are you clear on *how* the process of generational transfer can break down? And are you, together as one intergenerational leadership, collectively focused on the future while also respecting the values of the past?

In our context, what's fascinating these days is that a quarter century into one generational transfer, we're finding ourselves in the process of now starting another. And while our church is drastically different from the one founded in 1980 that transitioned leadership in the mid-90s, these same three questions undergird our process of identifying, involving, and empowering next generation leaders today as in previous eras. The only difference is that now I bear First Generation responsibilities instead of experiencing this process from a Second-Generation seat!

Today I pastor a community that includes not only my kids, but my parents and my in-laws. As our staff has expanded, I continue to lead together with friends like Michael and Chris. Our founding pastor still remains an active participant, along with his wife, children, grandchildren, and now great grandchildren! As we've grown and expanded, God has continued to breed in us the heart of a family—which has been so beautiful to experience, because the language of the church in the New Testament is far more of family than business. We're excited to see his spiritual family continue from generation to generation. And I'm excited to see the creativity and innovation the next generation brings to our community to help all of us continue *Finding Our Way*.

13

Female Leadership Development

As I described in our generational transfer journey in the previous chapter, when I started leading our church over two decades ago, our leadership was all male. A group of friends who'd grown up in the church, we were initially perceived by people as kind of a cute little band of brothers who were leading our church together. Fast-forward fifteen years or so, though, and people were starting to feel like we had instead become more of an impenetrable boys' club. A decade and a half into our era of leadership, our church still had no female elders, no regular female preachers, and no women on our senior leadership team.

To be clear: this was never our intent. From the time we started out in ministry, we theologically affirmed women in leadership. Personally, I always believed both men and women had gifts in leadership. Growing up, I saw leadership in my brother (who ended up pastoring with me for over fifteen years) and saw just as much leadership in my sister, who has run a Bible School in Japan for years. Even before settling on a theological position, my bias assumed that men and women ought to both be leading, and that the best leadership emerged when both men and women led together.

Conceding that, even today, the Christian church remains hotly divided over the role of women in ministry, I believe our experience and the learnings of this chapter can be helpful regardless of your church's view in this conversation, even to the most complementarian of views, since every church, regardless of its theology, still should care about loving and pastoring and including both genders well. The point of sharing our experience isn't to debate the role of women in the church, but merely to share our experience, where we assumed that, though we initially handed that leadership baton over to a group of young men as we transitioned our church's leadership to the next generation, things would normalize over the years. Yet after fifteen years of leading our church, nothing had happened, despite our best efforts and assumptions. Of the first three hires we ever made, two of them were women, and neither served in a role traditionally occupied by women (e.g., as assistants, in children's ministry, etc.). I assumed that, years into our ministry, gender would be an increasingly irrelevant fact in ministry, but that wasn't the case at all. A decade and a half into my ministry leadership, absolutely nothing had changed. What's worse is that we had absolutely no idea why.

A Woman to the Rescue!

I'd like to say that, at this point, one of us received some sort of spiritual enlightening from God. But sometimes when God wants to get something important done, he prefers to send a woman (like with announcing the resurrection)! In our case, he connected us with a leader from a camping ministry in northern Ontario named Ellen Duffield, who'd been doing research on female engagement and empowerment in the church.[1]

Boiling down Ellen's research into the two most significant points relevant to our context, she discovered that a woman's confidence level, on average, peaks at age nine. I'll say that again: as boys and girls grow up together, the confidence in women peaks—for their entire life—at the ripe old age of nine! From that point, through the influences of our larger society which then are typically exacerbated by the church, they journey along a trajectory that increasingly defaults to insecurity instead of confidence. Ellen would cite an example of a group of friends coming out of a college exam, where the guys would fist-pump over how they aced it—only to average 70 percent—where the women would fret about all the answers they weren't sure about only to average 95 percent. To be clear: this trajectory has nothing to do with competence; it has everything to do with confidence as women increasingly defaulted to insecurity.

Her second main finding had to do with what she labeled the "courts," the ideal environment in which someone thrived. Her research discovered that, in general, the male court was markedly different from the general female court. Like the difference between saltwater and freshwater fish,

---

1. You can find Ellen's book and additional study material at http://bravewomen.ca.

statistically speaking, men and women thrived in very different surroundings. Where men typically thrived on challenge, women typically thrived on affirmation. Men were driven by a desire to prove themselves, where women were motivated by being invited in. Where men thrived on debate and banter, women thrived by discovering their voice. Men liked to compete; women liked to collaborate. Ellen's research started to shed light on our blind spots of why we were failing to engage female leaders even though we wanted to: we were expecting women to thrive in a court that had been established around predominantly male dynamics. In short: we unknowingly were expecting women to thrive in a world built specifically for men.

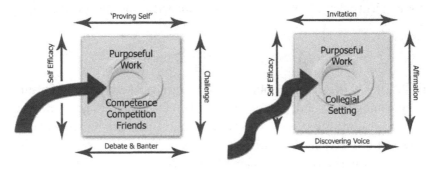

What Female Leadership Empowerment Looks Like

In response to Ellen's research, we acted on her recommendations in two strategic ways. First of all, in response to her research around the lack of confidence in women, we made a commitment to *disproportionate investment* into women's confidence and leadership. We launched two separate initiatives, one called "NextLEVEL Leadership" (NLL), which poured into two dozen of our most key female leaders over a two-year period of occasional retreats and regular small-group gatherings. The program focuses on biblical grounding, confidence-building, and voice-empowering leadership development initiatives. Every two years we launch another NLL initiative for another two dozen key leaders, while simultaneously adding the graduates of the previous cohort to our growing community of alumnae.

The other program we developed was an initiative specifically for sixth to eighth-grade girls—right at the genesis of that emerging erosion of confidence—that we now call "BRAVE Girls." It's organized into Year One, Two, and Three clusters, and each single year has a small handful of leaders devoted to it for the entire three-year run. As the years have now passed, there's also a growing group of graduated BRAVE Girl alumnae who, together with our NextLEVEL Leaders and alum, can serve as mentors and supports of this program. These two initiatives, including the gatherings, workshops, retreats, mentoring, and celebrations they include, have been the backbone to providing disproportionate investment into women.

In addition to this investment though, we responded to Ellen's research about the differences between the two courts. We wanted to create a leadership culture in which women could more easily thrive. To do that, in addition to the disproportionate investment into their confidence, we also sought to provide *disproportionate invitation*. We've been seeking to change the court of the culture of our work environment so that women don't have to live in a world built exclusively for men.

Specifically, when it comes to invitation, we're not only learning to actively reach out and invite women into leadership challenges and positions where they would have typically avoided stepping up (even though they had the competence). We've also been learning how to ongoingly invite women into conversations, to express their voice where they wouldn't naturally assert themselves or would be hesitant to compete for attention. Related to this, we've tried to be sensitive to research Ellen provided where any group would require a minimum of 30 percent female presence for women to feel comfortable expressing their voice. We've been seeking to increasingly create a culture that invites women in.

Nearly a decade into this adventure as a church, we certainly have a long way to go. But in the process of consistent years of disproportionate investment and disproportionate invitation, we've seen God move in some breathtaking ways. At the time of writing, we now have female elders and a female board chair. Our staff is now 50 percent women represented by a senior leadership that is comprised of 50 percent women. Women hold power and are visible role models. We're no longer seen—and more importantly, felt—as an impenetrable boys' club.

The Blessings of Diversity

And it's not just quantitative change. Around the same time we launched these initiatives, we started participating in a staff-wide employee engagement survey. That first year there was a stark difference in the experience of our men and women, with women scoring barely above the survey's statistical benchmark of "toxic." Our 2018 survey though, for the first time, scored women's experience of our workplace higher than men, far beyond the statistical threshold for "flourishing" (see Chapter 15). And it's not just the women who are benefitting. In total, that first employee engagement survey we conducted in 2013 registered our staff overall at the bare minimum of what they qualify as a healthy workplace, where now for the past two years we've registered in the top 1 percent of organizations to have ever taken the survey. As we actively pursue this vision of empowerment, described in our language as "spiritual moms and spiritual dads parenting the family together," our whole family is winning!

Here's the takeaway if you're a church leader, quoting Ellen Duffield herself: "Just because you don't *intend to exclude* doesn't mean you *intentionally include.*" As church leaders, we need to be honest about whether a vision of holistic leadership is being realized. We need to be sober about the blind spots of why what should happen isn't automatically happening. And we need to commit to deliberately doing different things and doing things differently in order to get different results instead of propagating the definition of insanity and continuing to do the same while expecting different.

The Influence of #MeToo and #ChurchToo

One of the powerful forces in our society in recent years has been the #MeToo movement, naming and protesting sexual harassment and assault of women. That influence has spread to shine a light on abuses and inequities in the church—designated by its own hashtag, #ChurchToo. And while the rectifying force of this movement has been profoundly positive in its protection and promotion of female leaders, there has been a shadow side. Bloomberg reported on how Wall Street has been responding to the #MeToo movement. Instead of citing growth in awareness of men and their behaviors, understandings of power dynamics or modifications of HR policies, the overwhelming solution seemed to be avoiding women altogether. No more one-on-one meetings. No more dinners. No sitting next to women on flights. Book hotel rooms on different floors. The article even referred to hiring women as "an unknown risk."

When it comes to the #ChurchToo version of this movement, I hope we can appreciate today that we find ourselves at an even more critical crossroads. I hear pastors all around the world these days reclaiming the "Billy Graham Rule" (whether they're even understanding or applying it properly), which has the potential to adversely affect all women in the church, and one woman most of all: The bride of Christ.

So, here are the bigger questions these days. Are we taking #MeToo and #ChurchToo seriously (because too many churches aren't)? And will taking #MeToo and #ChurchToo seriously stifle us from even asking the productive questions around female leadership empowerment? Will the fear in church leaders, especially male church leaders, especially senior church leaders, paralyze us from promoting the leadership potential of women in order to protect ourselves? What can we do in a time like this to not just avoid going backwards, but actually grow forwards in the empowerment and partnership of women in the church? How can we *both* protect *and* promote women? And, especially male senior church leaders, can we further grow in the Way of Jesus in the process, relinquishing our privilege for the sake of the women among us? Can we leverage our power to empower females to greater degrees of leadership?

There's more at stake than just women here. Last year the Canadian affiliate of Compassion International completed a succession plan for outgoing twenty-five-year president and CEO Barry Slauenwhite. In early 2018 they announced the president elect was a young female leader from our church named Allison Alley, who'd only started working at Compassion Canada six years earlier, just before participating in our first cohort of NextLEVEL Leadership. Children in poverty across the planet can benefit from empowered female leaders.

And closer to home I'm feeling it too. I have a daughter named Addilyn who recently entered sixth grade, which means she also got to join the Year One group of BRAVE Girls. After her first retreat, my wife Becky asked how it went, and Addy collapsed into her arms crying as she described a conversation with one of her mentor leaders. They'd been working through an exercise on your "inner voice," the critic inside you, and Addy said of this mentor she admired: "Her inner voice is even meaner than mine!"

I want my daughter Addy to know that she can become a person and leader like Allison. And I want our church to enjoy the full beauty and power of all of our spiritual moms and spiritual dads parenting our church family together. And I want our world to experience the fullness of both the maternal and paternal aspects of the heart of God.

So, I can't let the #MeToo and #ChurchToo movements cause me to shrink back. And neither can you. Church, and church leaders: don't let fear cripple your faith. For the sake of the bride of Christ, as we better protect women, let's promote them too!

14

LGBTQ+ Inclusion

IN 2005 I PREACHED my first message related to LGBTQ+ people and the church. Called "Church Eye for the Queer Guy," I brought out a set of boxing gloves as a prop to illustrate how contentious this subject was to discuss. Frankly, I didn't say much on the theology of marriage or sexuality. My focus was simply to try and create a space where we, as a local church family, could even have the capacity to talk about these things lovingly. If we could put the boxing gloves down, maybe God could do something.

What I didn't expect was that one of our church members would share the video of the message with a friend of theirs, a prominent gay man in our city who was an influential community voice for LGBTQ+ people. What I definitely didn't expect was him to like the talk and want to get together for lunch to chat further! Although somewhat anxious about what to expect (he could be quite contentious towards you if he didn't like you), I was thrilled with the opportunity to learn more about the LGBTQ+ community's perspective toward the Christian church. Our lunch conversation was congenial. He came to the conversation with a curiosity, as did I. Near the end, I asked him my bottom-line question: "If you could say one thing to the Christian church, what would it be?" As eager as I was to know, I wasn't prepared for his answer. Without skipping a beat, he replied, "I don't care what you believe; we've got to stop the suicides."

Two things struck me in that statement. The first was the harshness of the plight of many LGBTQ+ folks in their relationship to Christianity. One pastor friend who spent years forming a weekly small group with gay and lesbian members of their church learned, through hearing each of their stories, that virtually all of them always knew they were same-sex attracted from an early age. But because they were part of the church, they rejected that notion—tried to deny it—which only served to prove to them that they had discovered their innate same-sex attraction, as opposed to consciously choosing it. Because of their faith, they instantly and consistently tried to let God change it, what's often known as "praying the gay away," to no avail. Many shared stories of significant financial investments in therapies, re-treats, and medical approaches, none of which could change their sexual orientation. And—to a person—once they conceded they did, in fact, iden-tify as an LGBTQ+ person and couldn't change it, and no amount of faith or other strategies could allow them to escape it, they had all either considered or attempted to take their lives.

Yes, this issue is that serious. The impact of the Christian church's message on LGBTQ+ people is suicide-inducing shame. Facing that head-on in that lunch conversation was one of the most sobering moments of my ministry leadership life.

But there was a second factor to his response that equally shocked me. Aside from hearing the word "suicide," I was stunned to hear him use the word "we" as in "*we've* got to stop the suicides." From his perspective, without really knowing me, and certainly with no prior trust or credibility in what I belonged to, he considered us both, together, to be part of the solution. To him it was obvious that, beyond faith differences, our common humanity ought to unite us together to save lives and protect families. I left that lunch both humbled and convicted.

A Growing Problem

For the next number of years, our local church leadership began to stare that problem in the face: that the impact of the Christian church on the LGBTQ+ community has suicide-inducing consequences. At the very least, we could all agree that there was a serious impact problem here. The impact the Christian church was having, and is known to have, on the LGBTQ+ community was very different than the impact Jesus had on anyone when he walked the earth and taught about, and modeled, the kingdom of God. And since God was already breaking our hearts and awakening our minds to the realities of marginalization through the ministry of our Anchor Causes, our growing sensitivities made us want to, at the very least, be part of the solution to this problem we'd caused, and had awakened to, in our local church.

What we didn't realize then, though, was that this one problem is actually at least three problems—or at least three layers of problem. You see, the moment you declare you're seeking to address issues related to the exclusion of LGBTQ+ people in the church, you realize that everybody in the church holds fiercely strong opinions about these matters. The more we read and learned, the more we realized that, birthed out of theological interpretive roots, but often inflamed out of biases and even prejudices, these subjects carried a divisiveness and capacity for polarization like no other. One pastor referred to these issues as "radioactive" because of the intensity and vitriol of Christians towards one another in navigating them. But appreciating what we all know about God's heart for oneness and the unity of the body of Christ, this became a second layer to the problem we sought to address.

And it didn't stop there, because the combination of suicide-inducing marginalizing impact on the LGBTQ+ community, combined with the intense polarization and infighting of the Christian church over what to do about it, generated a third problem: the reputation of the church to the watching world. Of all the impressions unchurched people have of the Christian church these days—hypocritical, judgmental, and worthy of distrust—what frequently tops the list is "anti-gay." In this way, the church is most known by our surrounding society for what we're against—or, more importantly, *whom* we're against—instead of known for being *for* the people around us we're supposed to serve with the love of Jesus.

What Is Unity?

Staring this trifecta of challenges in the face, we sensed God leading us to concentrate on the second layer, the dividedness of believers on these matters. We wondered whether, if Christians could be more united in spite of different biblical perspectives on matters of marriage and sexuality, could we not both create the requisite safety for LGBTQ+ folks to explore, experience, and express faith in Jesus Christ, and at the same time paint a more compelling and credible picture to the watching world? Could unifying our church around these challenges be the key to unlocking all three layers of the problem?

For some reason though (again, trusting we were being prayerfully led by God's Spirit as a leadership), instead of asking which polarized side of the growing Christian divide we'd seek to unite our church around, we instinctively wondered: do all believers need to agree about all of this in order to be a church family together? In this chapter, I'm not going to unpack the theological differences between the two positions, what's often referred to in these theological discussions as the 'Side B' or traditional view (that restricts marriage to one man and one woman only, and restricts ministry to those who align in practice with those parameters), and the 'Side A' or affirming view (that permits marriage between LGBTQ+ people, and therefore permits all ministry opportunity to those faithfully covenanting together in that way). All we wondered was whether theological issues like the biblical definition of marriage were essential for all believers to agree on in order to function together as a Christ-centred spiritual family. Were shared beliefs on these interpretive matters prerequisite to being the church together?

Through these years of prayer, reflection, research, consultation, listening, and discernment, a few passages of Scripture stood out. One was the section of Paul's letter to the Roman church where he teaches on "disputable matters," issues of a non-salvation nature that had the potential to divide their community. You can read about them in Romans 14–15, where he highlights two polarizing issues in their day: observing Sabbaths and eating meat sacrificed to idols. There Paul encourages his readers to have personal convictions on these matters (i.e., don't just believe anything, or nothing) while resisting breaking fellowship over these disputable matters (even though these were Ten Commandment level, big deals in their day). Yet, his ultimate appeal is summarized in Romans 15:5–7, *"May the God who gives endurance and encouragement give you the same attitude of mind toward each other that Christ Jesus had, so that with one mind and one voice you may glorify the God and Father of our Lord Jesus Christ. Accept one another, then, just as Christ accepted you, in order to bring praise to God."* In spite of their fierce dividedness over these matters, and their strong urge to separate over them, Paul encourages them to actively foster one voice of unity and worship to Christ.

Have you ever considered the full implications of what this required? Non-meat-eaters viewed those who ate meat sacrificed to idols as flagrantly sinning against the law of God. Likewise, those who insisted on Sabbath-keeping were viewed as legalistically sinning against the freedom Jesus sought to bring. Rather than choosing one side or the other, in order for the Roman church to choose to function as one united voice of worship and service to Christ, they actually had to consciously choose to be the church together with people that, from their theological position, they believed were sinning. Not that Paul was encouraging believers to be soft on sin, but in the same way our world would interpret Jesus' clear teachings on wealth and material possessions differently around the globe, unity didn't require that everyone all believed the exact same thing or applied their beliefs in the exact same way.

Do you think the unity that Jesus prayed for among his people (see John 17:21–23) demanded that everyone believed the exact same things on what the Bible said about everything? If not, how could it be possible for someone to be united with someone they disagreed with? Maybe, we started wondering, in the simplicity and power of Jesus' prayer for oneness, it wasn't as conditional on sharing the same beliefs (especially on non-salvation matters) as we formerly assumed? Maybe his goal all along was for people of deep but diverse convictions on all sorts of faith matters to rise above their doctrinal differences and unite their hearts, minds, and lives around something grander: the person, life and love, death and resurrection of Jesus himself. Especially when you consider the primacy of the Law of Love in Jesus' teaching framework (discussed in greater detail back in Chapter 6), maybe theological uniformity wasn't to be our church's highest calling, but unity was?

Understandably, this messed with us for a while. Wouldn't we be wishy-washy if we tolerated multiple views on such important topics? How would that lack of singular clarity disciple a next generation looking for answers to life's tough questions? We worried that these issues were just too big to treat secondarily in our community, until we reflected further. Another significant passage was the response of Jesus to the Sadducees' challenge of the resurrection, where they ask which husband a woman would have in heaven after she had been married to seven different brothers in the course of her life on earth. Among other places recorded in the Gospels, Jesus responded this way in Luke 20:34–35, *"The people of this age marry and are given in marriage. But those who are considered worthy of taking part in the age to come and in the resurrection from the dead will neither marry nor be given in marriage."* His response is: marriage isn't really an eternal matter. So, we had to ask ourselves: if our mission as a local church is to usher in the realities of the kingdom of God on earth as it is in heaven, and in heaven marriage doesn't appear to be a matter of lasting significance, why are we treating these debates about marriage as though they are the most important conversation in the church? Could issues like this actually be matters where we could foster unity amidst a theological diversity, offering one voice of worship and service to Jesus in spite of fiercely divided perspectives that would otherwise lead us to separate from each other?

Love Beyond Belief

We collectively felt as a local church leadership, that this may be the most significant point at which we were called to live out the biblical value of what we refer to as "Love Beyond Belief," the primacy of the Law of Love that supersedes other theological issues. So, at Southridge, we've sought to unite our community of diverse beliefs on these matters as a single, mutually respectful and submissive family. We're actively fostering the capacity for people who hold Side A affirming views to be the church together with people who hold Side B traditional views, as incompatible as those views may seem. We're seeking to be a family together, even though our views cause us to feel and perceive that others in our community, because of their views and their willingness to live them with integrity, are sinning.

At a policy level, while holding to the corporate conviction of a traditional definition of marriage, which, aligned with our denomination, is the only definition of marriage that gets publicly taught and corporately practiced, we simultaneously respect those who hold the alternative view. And that respect goes beyond sentiment in that, outside of the most senior leadership roles (where denominational alignment is required), someone with an affirming view is included and involved in ministry, without having to hide or compromise their view. They're free, and actively encouraged, to serve and lead as part of our community. And they're welcomed in as active, contributing, influential members of our community, free to live out their affirming view through LGBTQ+ marriage. While we don't perform LGBTQ+ marriages, we embrace and include those who hold that theological view.

Objection!

Obviously, this position doesn't track with everyone (another way in which the church holds multiple convictions!). But it's been remarkable to see the wide bandwidth of Christ followers God has united among us who are eager to engage in his mission together across these theological divides. Put bluntly: do people who hold an affirming view feel our church is oppressive to some degree? Absolutely. And do people who hold a traditional view feel LGBTQ+ marriage and allowing LGBTQ+ married couples active membership in our community is immoral to some degree? Absolutely. But more than their convictions on these theological matters, they're bound together by the Spirit of Christ, as a matter of greater weightiness than these theological matters. And, more importantly, they are bound together by what is the ultimately most important and unifying dynamic, that of receiving and sharing Christ's love. They recognize each other as siblings in Christ. And, as we unify amidst our diverse doctrinal positions on marriage and sexuality, we're not only painting a picture of oneness that's becoming compelling to our surrounding society, we're creating a safe place where LGBTQ+ people and their families can know, with confidence, that Southridge isn't just a place that welcomes them to attend, but is legitimately a family where they can belong to fully explore, experience, and express faith in Christ as part of our church family.

I assume this position likely doesn't track with you either. And I know the risk of including this chapter. Appreciating that a few pages of summary will never capture the full nuance of a decade and a half of God's leading among us, I'm hoping that sharing even the high points of our processing is helpful and not detrimental to you and your church's journey of *Finding Our Way*. Appreciating this conversation is as much a hermeneutical one (about how you interpret the Scriptures), my goal isn't for you to agree with our church's leadership; it's only to get you to ask tough questions you may not want to deal with but, for Jesus' sake, our churches desperately need to face. The goal is to inspire churches to have the same impact on LGBTQ+ people that Jesus had on everybody, which is not commonly their current experience among us. As the journey of *Finding Our Way* continues, this only becomes one more layer of relinquishing privilege for those of less privilege. Considering that the legacy of Jesus' impact was comfort to the legitimately afflicted, often to the affliction of the legitimately comfortable, how much discomfort are you willing to embrace in order to create genuine welcome and inclusion of LGBTQ+ people in your church community?

If you feel like lowballing the significance of these theological issues waters down the gospel, have a fresh read of Paul's letter to the Galatians where he reminds them that adding any supplementary theological requirements to the "by grace alone, through faith alone, in Christ alone" way of Jesus is actually watering down grace! More than that, appreciate that these issues aren't issues—they're *people*, made in God's image to be loved and cherished by him. Appreciate that the definition of insanity is doing the same thing but expecting different results and ask what you're willing to change in order to change the three-layered impact problem the Christian church faces these days.

Could we at least commit to putting down the boxing gloves? From my perspective, I don't care what you believe—we've got to stop the suicides, together.

15

Organizational Culture

OF ALL THE CHANGES you can make in your church on the journey of *Finding Our Way*, there's one that matters more than all the others: the culture of your organization. I didn't always appreciate or believe in the importance of culture. But as I reflect on the past two decades and recall all the ways God has been revolutionarily transforming our lives and community, the way he's fundamentally changed our staff and workplace culture among our ministry leaders has not only been the most significant; it's been the most critical. Every church and ministry leader values culture, and every leader at some level seeks to be a culture-changer. But I wonder how many of us really appreciate that focusing on culture is the single most vital thing a Christian leader can do. And, more practically, I wonder how many of us really understand the strategies and practicalities around what it actually takes to change a culture for the better.

Reflecting on our experiences, I can see at least six critical stages of appreciating and valuing culture that I've personally journeyed through as a leader. Each of these have corresponded to some practical commitments towards cultural change. So, this chapter seeks to walk us through the six convictions, or, maybe more accurately, the six stages of conviction God has grown in me when it comes to valuing a leader's focus on culture and cultural change.

Culture Gets Work Done

The first would have been after a number of years of leading in my church, where in those early years all we were fixated on was strategy, on how to do things. In that era of metamorphosis, churches like ours were revisiting how we did pretty much everything: how to do weekend services, how to disciple people and integrate them into community, how to do local and global mission, how to serve kids and reach students. And I mention this only because, even now, most people who work in churches primarily care about these things, the issues of *strategy* related to doing their work.

Then one day a few years into my ministry life I heard Patrick Lencioni say that "Culture eats strategy for breakfast." It was the first time I'd given any conscious thought to something other than vision or strategy. But the deeper I dug into his books, the more I realized that the very vision you dream about fulfilling, that gets realized through the very strategy you're promoting, gets exponentially enhanced or diminished depending on your culture. So, we started to formalize work plans and, in Lencioni's language, "Rally Cries." We translated those work plans into weekly schedules and areas of focus. We began to provide regular check-ins on those work plans, as well as seasonal areas of focus, through a recurring rhythm of one-on-one performance management. On top of that, we took steps to establish some formalized team dynamics, beyond just intermittent catchups when we felt like we needed to talk. We initiated regular update meetings, strategy sessions, and semi-annual off-sites. We started to attend to the dynamics of culture building.

And wouldn't you know it, that attention to culture started to catalyze our strategy. Our weekend services were getting better, ministry leaders were delivering on goals, local and global outreach initiatives were launched. We started learning the most basic lesson: that you need to focus on culture to get work done. Culture eats strategy for breakfast.

Culture Gets Church Work Done

So, at that point, things around our church really started to pick up as our culture was starting to drive our strategy, that is, until we started experiencing issues of ineffectiveness and underperformance among some of our leaders. Then, in our performance management conversations, there started to be accountabilities applied, and in some cases instances of discipline or repositioning and, at times, even dismissal. This is where we learned the hard way about the unique challenges of ministry work.

This one is a bit more theological. In the book of Romans, the apostle Paul appears to be building a case for how the gospel works. Specifically, he seems to be contrasting the grace-based system of Jesus with the works-based system of the religion. As he's building this contrast, he says in Romans 4:4, *"When people work, their wages are not a gift, but . . ."* and then goes on to contrast employment dynamics with the beauty and power of the free gift of salvation made available to all of us through Jesus.

What took me years to appreciate, though, was the biblical affirmation that, when people work, their wages are not a gift. What I never realized was how contrary the values of employment are with the values of the gospel. And what I never understood was that vocational church ministry work was so challenging because both the works-based system of employment and the grace-based system of the gospel were at play.

In kingdom work, and specifically, church employment, people are *both* loved unconditionally *and* paid conditionally. Relationships are *both* covenantal *and* contractual. Employees are to be *both* fully loved *and* fully judged or assessed. Your employment value is a result of what you do, but your Christian value is based on what Christ has done. This became a huge cultural analysis for us, to get church work done. We had to learn how to navigate *both* the works-based system of employment *and* the grace-based system of ministry.

Culture Gets Church Work Done Together

Then, as our ministry progressed, we ran into another problem: people who didn't fit. At the time, I didn't understand that this is what was happening. All I knew was that, from time to time, things wouldn't be working out, even though the employee was generally godly and competent. There was some kind of elusive intangible that we couldn't put a finger on.

Starting to increasingly see our world through cultural lenses, we created an exercise that occupied the entire two days of an off-site senior leadership retreat. Every leadership team member had to present to the group the person (outside of our team!) whom they felt was the best example of who we are as an organization, the best fit. In addition, each person had to suggest the person in our organization they felt was the worst fit. In addition to presenting these names, they had to also provide rationale as to why they chose them.

The results were fascinating. Of the half dozen people sharing, only two names were suggested as the best fits and only two names were suggested as the worst. There was tremendous consensus. More to that, the reasons were very similar, and the reasons for the best fits were the virtual inverse of the reasons for the worst. We took an entire afternoon to mine out the common themes of these reasons, and after an additional session to wordsmith the summaries we came up with five cultural distinctives of our workplace: we're *fanatically collaborative* (believing we're better together), we're *never satisfied* (always aspiring to improve), we *totally own this* (work from an owner mentality as opposed to just punching the clock and doing the bare minimum required), we're *oriented to outsiders* (and somewhat averse to evangelical Christian subculture) and we "*go there*" (unafraid to address the "final 3 percent" of crucial conversations).

Presenting this to our staff was a breath of fresh air, affirming to those who fit the culture, clarifying to others as to how they could better fit the culture, and liberating to those who didn't fit the culture. Since then, this filter not only gets reinforced, it's also become an entire phase of focus in our hiring process. Focusing on these cultural distinctives has enabled us to get church work done together. It provides alignment around the elusive intangibles.

Culture Engages People

Well by now, we were becoming culture fanatics, when all of a sudden we heard about a staff workplace culture assessment tool at the Global Leadership Summit from an organization called BCWI: The Best Christian Workplaces Institute. We decided to take a crack at this thing and have our entire staff complete the fifty-five-question survey. Each question was ranked on a scale of one to five, from "strongly disagree" to "strongly agree." Once the results were tallied, we discovered that we were barely a healthy organization. When I say, "barely healthy," I mean that we literally scored 4.00 on that first survey, the statistical bare minimum threshold for organizational health. Someone called it "skin of your teeth" level healthy. And it made us look in the mirror again at our workplace culture.

Suffice to say, every single year we've done the BCWI employee engagement survey and follow-up consultation has identified a small handful of the good, bad, and ugly truths about our staff culture, naming the greatest weaknesses in our workplace culture. So, we took what we call a "bottleneck approach" to address the greatest hindrances to a flourishing culture each year. One year it was pay and benefits, another year it was our on-boarding process. One year we focused on teamwork and training. This past year we focused on having more fun, which is harder than you think when you're no fun! Every year we focused our energies on improving the two or three statistically worst things about our culture, which year after year devotes our attention to new worst things while cumulatively improving and strengthening our culture and our people's experience in it.

In the eight years we've deployed the survey instrument, we've gone from 4.00 to exceeding, and now oscillating around, 4.50. For the past four years, we've surveyed in the top 1 percent of all BCWI churches who've ever been surveyed. And best of all, in some years every single one of our departments live above the 4.25 threshold for flourishing. In this regard, we've learned that focusing on your workplace culture gets church work done together through engaged people. And the difference in engagement between people driving into the parking lot at 4.00 compared to 4.50 is, as Mark Twain said, "the difference between a lightning bug and lightning." There's no comparison.

Culture's Greatest Gift

These four lessons are, in many ways, what the past fifteen or so years of awakening to the importance of organizational culture has taught us. But over that time, kind of as one big cumulative lesson, we've also learned a fifth value to focusing on culture. And of all the "ahas" we've had, this one is by far the most significant.

It started when we were first discovering the concept of a workplace culture, when we were humbled to realize something we'd never even considered before. It developed as we revisited Scripture to make sense of the unique complexities of the coexisting systems of works and grace that are unique to vocational ministry. It further deepened when we clarified our unique cultural distinctives, getting honest with ourselves about who we were and who we weren't, and who we distinctly sought and ought to be. It strengthened as a result of the annual feedback and accountability of the BCWI instrument. And it intensified all the more as we repented of our blind ignorance in the ways we'd been stifling the female leaders among us (which I described in detail in Chapter 13). This particular value didn't emerge through any one specific initiative or era. It was the cumulative effect of all of them.

What value am I talking about? What value develops through being humbled, through revisiting the Scriptures, through getting honest with yourself, through feedback and accountability, and through repentance? This isn't an organizational value, per se. This is the value of spiritual growth that is both required for, and results from, caring about and allowing yourself to be shaped into the kind of people that precipitate a genuinely healthier culture. For years, I'd been awakened to the significance of paying attention to and strengthening your culture, but it's only in very recent years that I've had the spiritual eyes to see the depth and significance with which God, by his Spirit, has been able to form Jesus Christ in us as a staff and church leadership through it.

At one level, you just can't fake cultural change, especially over a long period of time. Things don't become safer and more honest, more encouraging and supportive, quicker to resolve conflicts cleanly, or more eager to celebrate wins without some serious heart-level work among your teammates. BCWI survey questions like, "My supervisor cares about me as a person" don't improve through an action plan alone. They require the inside-out supernatural working of the Holy Spirit within people to grow and generate a greater degree of his fruit: love, joy, peace, patience, kindness, goodness, faithfulness, gentleness, and self-control. True, lasting cultural change only happens when there's significant, supernatural personal change in leaders.

When that kind of change is happening though, something else happens. Now, when the spiritual leaders of a community are, especially over time, demonstrating bona fide transformation and growth in their capacity to resemble the character of Jesus, they gain integrity. Now, the marketplace-working congregants that they're inviting into expressing who Jesus is at their workplaces are being invited into that adventure by leaders who are doing and demonstrating the very same thing. Now, leaders of faith communities are practising the very thing they're preaching to others.

And when that happens, people outside faith communities benefit as well. Not only do coworkers of these marketplace Christ followers enjoy more of Jesus through their changing lives and workplaces, but in some sense the very suspicions that underlie our watching world, things like the church being judgmental, hypocritical, or worthy of distrust (described in earlier chapters), start to be reversed. As people see and celebrate the spiritual growth at the epicentre, that transformation, shared about and passed through leaders to others, slowly substitutes that negative stereotype for one of warm embrace, credibility, and trustworthiness in people.

And then . . . we've come full circle. We started a journey of appreciating the value of focusing on culture because it gets work done. But what's the real work of the church, and frankly, of any Christian-based ministry or organization? It's not just to implement its strategies and drive its programs with greater effectiveness, especially since culture eats strategy for breakfast. The goal of Christ-centred organizations is to reveal Jesus to the world around it, and to usher in the realities of the kingdom of God on earth as it is in heaven. That's the "work" that any church or ministry ultimately exists to do. And you can't really do that work without primarily focusing on your organization's culture.

Attending to your workplace culture, then, is actually the organizational equivalent of "self-leadership." A leader can only take people where they've been. A leader can only provide spiritually for others what is flowing out of the activity of God within them. The same thing's true for a community. After years of being convinced of the importance of attending to our workplace culture, it's only in the past couple of years that I've grasped the reality that culture is the single most important thing in any ministry, because of my deepest conviction: focusing on culture allows you to experience the kingdom of God on earth as it is in heaven. Attending to your culture is the process of personally becoming more like Christ as you do the work of Christ where you are.

If you're eager to get work done better, together, through engaged people, by realizing their potential, there's actually something even more important that you should focus on. All of these convictions around culture matter. But please, for Jesus' sake, do not let yourself miss out on the greatest gift that focusing on your culture can give you. The starting point for building a church that resembles Jesus to a greater degree is becoming a person and leader who's growing in *your* resemblance of Jesus. More than casting vision, building teams, and developing strategies, becoming more like Jesus and ushering in the reality of the kingdom in your heart and the hearts of those around you is what kingdom leaders exist to do!

Discerning Our Way

Looking to the Future

As a local church pastor, one of my greatest pet peeves is when leaders at conferences, in books, or on podcasts say, "The church *should*. . . ." I find that so frustrating because idealistically pointing out what leaders like me *should* be doing, while aspirational, is pragmatically unhelpful. When I hear from a leader, I don't want to hear what they think I *should* be doing; I want to hear *how* they are addressing that issue or implementing that change so I can learn from them *how* I can incorporate their experiences into our ministry and leadership in practical ways.

So far, I hope that by sharing our local church's thinking on how we understand God's vision, mission, and outcome, and by outlining our experiences of trying to implement those ideas into an operationalized ministry, has given you something to work with beyond stating what you *should* be doing. I hope you've benefitted from some of the investment of God's activity in our church community over the past quarter century by discovering *how* a local church can make some productive changes in its ministry to shift the impact to the watching world from hypocritical, judgmental, and worthy of distrust to a reputation of integrity, welcome, and inclusion, and respected credibility.

That said, there are some additional aspects to the journey of *Finding Our Way* where, as a leadership, we have thoughts, questions, and ideas, but haven't yet actualized them into our operationalized system of ministry. Since these tend to be commonly discussed issues of significant importance to the life, health, and especially the future, of the Christian church, I wanted to at least share our perspectives to stimulate your own reflections. So, while these next chapters won't necessarily provide examples of *how*, hopefully they will reveal what the church *could* become, instead of just annoying you with one more church leader telling you what you *should* be doing.

16

Leveraging Technology

THIS IS PROBABLY THE single most difficult chapter for me to write, and not just because I'm not terribly tech savvy or because I'm quite social media averse. I'm writing this in the middle of the COVID-19 pandemic, where the church has "pivoted to online" by leveraging technology. With this seismic shift has come tidal waves of pundits who are predicting what life post-pandemic will look like. In the networks I'm connected to, much of that predicting has to do with whether the church will learn to permanently adapt to the emerging digital age. The assumption is that the Christian church, typically lagging behind the pace of society, will finally get with the program of going virtual and, post-COVID, be smart enough to not regress. Most futurists are crediting the pandemic for finally pole-vaulting the church into the digital age.

In my experience though, that's not what I'm seeing during this pandemic at all. In fact, I would flatly disagree with the assumption that the church's future is online. This has forced me to reflect on where the strength of those feelings is coming from, and I hope I can articulate them in a balanced way that is at least aware of my bias. To be clear: I believe the church has tremendous potential to leverage technology, but I feel that some of the greatest threats the church faces today are also due to its pursuit of leveraging technology. And while I one day may embarrassingly regret ever including this chapter, my feelings on this subject are too strong to let it go completely unaddressed in our journey together of *Finding Our Way*.

What We Know

For starters, it's probably worth clarifying a couple of realities that are hope-fully obvious. First, technology itself is neither good nor bad. Technology is inanimate, merely a set of tools that extend the capacities already possessed by people, so it's not simple nor reasonable to apply a blanket for-all-times label of morality to it. Second, the Scriptures would provide both pros and cons to the theory of whether to leverage technology for the advancement of the purposes of God (some of which I've included in this chapter). When it comes to playing our part in God's enduring story throughout human history, technology can be both an opportunity and a threat to fulfilling God's mission and realizing his vision for his church.

On the one hand, we need to appreciate that the *content* of the mes-sage can be communicated virtually. The Good News of Jesus Christ does not require direct in-person, face-to-face contact in order for God's power to work through it. If that were the case, the Bible would be of little use to believers—as its content is also communicated through a technological medium (as is this book about the church!). Think about how the apostle Paul continued to spread the good news of Jesus even while under house arrest. Known as the "prison epistles," Paul could leverage the technology of letter-writing to communicate to his hearers, as in Colossians 4:18, *"I, Paul, write this greeting in my own hand. Remember my chains. Grace be with you."* For sure, Paul longed to be face-to-face with his hearers again, but knew he could lean into current technology in order to continue seeing the gospel of Jesus Christ spread. For a fact, you do not need to be present with your audience for the message of God to connect into human heads and hearts. Technology can help magnify God's message.

At the same time, we also need to appreciate that the *medium* of God's message cannot be translated virtually. This is because the good news of Jesus Christ isn't just content; it's the risen life of the person of Jesus! As he described in John 10:10, *"The thief comes only to steal and kill and destroy; I have come that they may have life, and have it to the full."* Jesus came to earth and lived, died, and rose again to spiritually empower people to experience the abundant life God had originally designed humanity to enjoy, and to unify believers together to share and spread that life to others as a restor-ative force around their world. The message of Jesus isn't just a message; it is his life experienced, trusted in, received, enjoyed, and shared. So instead of leveraging the technology of the day to send a message to the world, Jesus had to actually *enter into it incarnationally* to become human so his life could be lived in and through his followers. The essence of the gospel, not just the content of it, isn't mere words but a person to be experienced. Even in the wake of his ascension, Jesus left behind a "body" to be the continuing incarnation of his presence in the world: the church. The gospel is not just informational, or even inspirational, but *incarnational*; meaning the gospel can only be fully responded to, embraced, and embodied in the crucible of real life, opposed to being consumed online.

This is where I see limits to the church's capacity to leverage technology. As discussed in Chapter 7, to teach or communicate the content about the life of Jesus is one thing, for which technology can be liberally leveraged, but to experience the vibrancy of his resurrection life requires just that: experience. Only the incarnational life of Jesus can change a human heart, and since God's Plan A for living out Jesus' legacy was his people, there's a critical life-on-life, face-to-face, word becoming flesh component for the people of God to be used by God to both experience his life and love and to share it with others. Relying exclusively on technology will spread content but will often fail to share the experience of his life and love that our surrounding society so desperately needs.

How frustrating would it be if a couple went to marriage counselling, in dire straits with little hope, and the counsellor simply tossed them a book to read? While the counsellor may believe strongly in the content of the book, the couple requires more than just content to de-tangle their marital mess. They need perspective and advice, prayer and encouragement. They need ongoing accountability and support. In short: they need the incarnated life and love of the counsellor, and a community—and through their presence, Jesus—not just the content of his good news.

Even as we navigate the COVID-19 pandemic, I'm struck by how "digital" some leaders assume the church ought to become in the future. People are losing their jobs and struggling financially, but there's no technology that's going to instantaneously put food on their table. People wrestling with aloneness can't satiate that struggle with an app. To meet the needs of the homeless, hurting, or hungry requires actually physically meeting them. You can't house or feed someone digitally; they require the actual, tangible, practical support provided through the incarnational life and love of Jesus. While there are apps that perform many of these functions, and can be useful in extreme circumstances, they are no replacement for participation in a community that exudes the life and love of Jesus.

The Technological Challenge

To me, this opens up once again the conversation of what it means for the Christian church to be culturally relevant. The assumption that the church of the future will more permanently shift to digital follows the logic flow of the marketplace. Fifty years ago, small shops and stores were predominantly replaced by the one-stop-shopping of big box stores. This was paralleled in the church by the emergence of the megachurch phenomenon, where people could experience the most comprehensive and quality programming in the most convenient and accessible ways. Nowadays though, that same logic sees big box stores being replaced by online outlets like Amazon, accessing the convenience of online shopping, or take-out apps instead of actually dining at a restaurant. And once again, so goes the logic, since society is headed in that direction (greater convenience and accessibility from home), the church ought to follow suit if it's going to remain culturally relevant.

I don't disagree at all with that logic flow. What I'm fundamentally opposed to is applying the values of consumerism directly to the ministry of the Christian church (as should have been evident throughout this entire book). Just because the consumer markets are headed in a certain direction does not mean the church must immediately or fully follow suit. In fact, many times God desires quite the opposite. In Romans 12:2 Paul writes, *"Do not conform to the pattern of this world, but be transformed by the renewing of your mind. Then you will be able to test and approve what God's will is—his good, pleasing and perfect will."* Similar to 1 John 2, where the adage of "being in the world but not of the world" emerges, God challenges believers to carefully discern in what ways they ought to make the most of societal customs and in what ways they specifically ought to function counter-culturally.

So, on the one hand, defining the future of the church as predominantly digital fails to consider what exactly you're inviting people into. As most churches did, for example, because of the pandemic, our church "pivoted" its weekend services to an online form. From my perspective, the experiences we offered were quite good. More than that, they were very well received. We saw people, during this pandemic, sharing them with their friends beyond our church and hearing stories (which our increased online views confirm) of curious people leveraging the opportunity of the convenience and privacy of their own homes to check out Southridge. This excites me and makes me wonder how we can continue to leverage technology to further reach into where people outside of faith are starting from. At the same time, though, it scares me, because from a consumerism perspective we're reinforcing that the Christian church is something someone is able to access through our online experience as a point-and-click opportunity, when in fact the root of responding to Jesus' invitation to follow him is through devotion, not consumerism.

On the other hand, I'm also uncomfortable with the medium-that-is-the-message sent to people through our online experience. Again, in the coronavirus pandemic this may be unavoidable, but for people accessing our weekend services online, they're drawing a Sunday-centric conclusion about a life of faith. Even easier than reducing a lifestyle of full devotion to mere churchgoing, now people can reduce it to church-watching. Through the medium of playing a video over the internet, we run the risk of communicating a greater message than the topics of our Sunday morning sermons: we subconsciously (and more formatively) communicate that faith is something to be watched as a spectator. This posture may be appropriate for seekers, people with no professed faith commitment, as they explore the possibility of faith, but as I've argued this is not the posture of devotion to Christ. As discussed in the bulk of the first sections of this book, passivity and inactivity rooted in consumerism that reduces Church to an hour on Sundays, I believe, is a huge cause for the disconnect in people's impressions of Jesus followers versus their opinions of Jesus. Particularly, this contributes strongly to the tendency towards hypocrisy, because all we've done in leading our people is provided them something stimulating to watch instead of activating them to behave more like Jesus.

The Deeper Challenges

On top of that basic challenge though—effectively communicating the medium of Jesus' risen life and love through inanimate digital technology—there seem to be further perils the more the church leverages technology to stimulate faith. Consider, for example, the ways the church has embraced social media as a communication tool. At Southridge, we seek to leverage platforms like Facebook, Twitter, and Instagram to get information out to people all the time. In fact, social media has become our primary way to promote the events and activities around our community.

The reason that is, though, is because the primary product social media platforms sell is self-promotion. (Even when it is leveraged towards other ends, self-promotion is still inherent in the medium, which *is* the message.) While we leverage it to promote our church's happenings, by using a technology designed for self-promotion we're also silently reinforcing the use of technology for self-promotion. But is a life of self-promotion anywhere close to the character or teaching of Jesus? Jesus taught to do your good deeds in secret, not to take a photograph and post it online, as though otherwise it didn't happen. Jesus voluntarily relinquished his divine privileges and made himself nothing, and we as his followers are to, as Paul teaches in Philippians 2:3–5, do likewise, *"Do nothing out of selfish ambition or vain conceit. Rather, in humility value others above yourselves, not looking to your own interests but each of you to the interests of the others. In your relationships with one another, have the same mindset as Christ Jesus."* Jesus self-consciously made decisions that cost him thousands of followers, as in John 6:66. The life of a Jesus follower is defined by humility, others-orientation, and servitude, which seem to be the opposite values upon which social media is built.

More than the example though, I'm concerned with the net impact (pardon the pun!). Even pre-COVID, mental health issues like anxiety and depression were at all-time highs. And many of these dynamics have been directly linked to an increase in social media use. By constantly constructing your online presence, commonly known as "building your brand," life is being reduced for many to perception-generation instead of being lived authentically through transparency, vulnerability, and accountability in community. Not only are people being reduced to avatars, we're also being forced into the comparison game as we constantly scroll the highlight reels of people's lives on our social media feeds. Then, as the compulsion for comparison or receiving "likes" increases, it becomes increasingly difficult to let go of or turn off our devices, resulting in excessive use, workaholism, and screen addiction. In addition, though it doesn't have to be this way, social media has contributed to the problem of polarization in our culture through the anger and hate that inspired the internet wisdom, "Never read the comments." I'm sure to some of you I'm sounding like a real killjoy, but are we as church leaders pressing pause long enough to ask ourselves what as a society we're becoming and comparing that to the way of Jesus we're invited into? And have we accurately assessed both the opportunities and threats of leveraging technology to advance his Way of Life in the world around us?

At Southridge, we leverage technology for our ministry. I wouldn't profess that we leverage it well, nor would I claim to know what leveraging it well necessarily means. For example, we leverage prerecorded video messages at all of our location's weekend services (except one, as the live teacher rotates through each location week-to-week), so we were able to pivot our services to online quite seamlessly. Like I said earlier, we're growing in our frequency of communicating key updates through social media channels. We even have a Southridge app, which we hope can help further foster the lifestyle of full devotion. The guiding principle, in our case though, is whether leveraging technology is the *means to the end* or if it has become the *end itself*, where tech engagement trumps life transformation. We are trying to discern the line between using the tool of technology and giving in to the tyranny of technology. That's the tightrope we're trying to navigate when it comes to leveraging technology.

Our end is about more than propagating a message, it's propagating an experience of real (as opposed to virtual) life. To function effectively as a Holy Spirit-empowered, unified force of restoration in the world requires us to increasingly propagate the way of life of Jesus: his in-spiritedness, his relational connectedness, and his social action advocating for compassion and justice. To that end, there is no technology that can replace the risen life and power of the person of Jesus, which is always only fully communicated life-on-life. As a means to that end, if there are ways we can leverage technology to magnify our capacity—from the printing press, to the automobile, to the internet—we'll try to, while at the same time seeking to be realistic about the medium that is the message of leveraging certain technology and what we're modeling for our people as we do. Hopefully, the challenge of the apostle Paul in 1 Corinthians 7:31 can be our guide, *"Those who use the things of the world should not become attached to them. For this world as we know it will soon pass away."*

In an increasingly technological age, we're hoping to use technology to advance God's kingdom without allowing technology to use us. Our goal is to continue to creatively leverage digital as a means to the much greater end of increasing people's experience of the incarnational. Our hope is to invite people into a fully devoted way of life, not just a one-hour experience they can increasingly enjoy from the convenience and comfort of their home. And more than being known as the "hip" or "cool" church because of how we're leveraging technology, we're desperate to be known as the "legit" church who makes sense of Jesus because we're trading in the world's impressions of hypocrisy for integrity, judgmentalism for legitimate welcome and inclusion, and societal distrust for respected credibility. In that regard, while I'm far from tech savvy, you could say that, at Southridge, we're trying to leverage technology to be in our world but not of it.

I hope our use of technology is helping us become more culturally relevant than ever!

17

Denominations and Church Partnerships

Denominations have never made sense to me. When I first started in leadership at our local church, I realized I was part of inheriting not only our immediate church family's relationships, but also those of our extended church family through our denomination. Growing up, I participated in our denomination's summer camp, but didn't attend our denomination's high school, so I had some exposure but wasn't completely familiar with it. Soon though, I had become a delegate at our denomination's annual convention, and after a few years served on our denomination's Leadership Council. None of these types of experiences, though, could help me get my head around why Christian denominations even exist.

On one level, I could see that our denomination, like many, was entangled with a particular ethnicity and/or cultural heritage. People would introduce themselves by making reference to known relatives, so the rest of the group could place them in the family tree where they fit and play the game of figuring out how they were related. While I couldn't participate from a family of origin perspective, since I married someone from the ethnic group represented by our denomination, I could easily shift gears into my wife's world and play the game. From this perspective, certain terms and language, and even certain foods, seemed to define our denomination as much as any doctrine or ministry we offered.

At another level, I could trace back our denomination to the influence of a specific leader, from whom our denomination originated. Like *Calvin*ists or *Luther*ans, our denomination—the *Menno*nite Brethren—originated from the influence of Menno Simons, a voice in the Anabaptist tradition of Christianity. This influence seemed to represent some of the distinction between ours and other area churches that otherwise felt similar to ours. While we offered similar styles of services and similar kinds of ministry, this helped explain what was fundamentally different about us.

Related to that, our denomination, like many others, was circumscribed by a Confession of Faith. What was interesting, especially in my earlier days when I was first being credentialed and ordained as a minister within the Conference of Mennonite Brethren Churches, was that the main features of our denomination's faith statement were essentially no different than most other Bible-believing, Christ-following denominations, but woven within their practices were some critically-core distinctives. I discovered, for example, that the primary difference between our denomination and that of a close mentor church of ours was that, while both Anabaptists, practicing believer's baptism by immersion, the other denomination baptized three times and forward (in the name of the Father, Son, and then Holy Spirit), while ours baptized backwards and only once. Yet, we remained two distinct groups, rather than being united into one.

In the year 2000, the Centre for the Study of Global Christianity at Gordon-Conwell Theological Seminary estimated that there were approximately thirty-four thousand Christian denominations across the planet. By 2012 they estimated that number had grown to approximately forty-three thousand. Have you been able to make sense of why that is?

Biblically Based?

Denominations have never made sense to me, because when I look at the teachings of the New Testament, in the era of restoration in God's story where we find ourselves today, not only do I not find the existence of denominations, I also actually see the New Testament writers (especially the Apostle Paul) specifically encouraging the Church to *not* subdivide or identify in the ways today's denominations seem to.

Take, for example, Paul's teaching in Galatians 3:28, *"There is neither Jew nor Gentile, neither slave nor free, nor is there male and female, for you are all one in Christ Jesus."* What happens when someone experiences saving faith in Jesus is that they receive a new identity, not just that they're made alive when they were formerly spiritually lifeless, but that they now belong to God's spiritual family, where they were formerly outsiders. And that spiritual family identifies all believers in Jesus as one. In Christ, members of the family of God subjugate distinctives like their ethnic heritages to embrace their higher calling and identity as the one family of God through Jesus.

Similarly, Paul rebuked believers in the Corinthian church because they were subdividing according to their loyalties and allegiances to human leaders in their community. He writes in 1 Corinthians 3:3–4, *"You are still worldly. For since there is jealousy and quarreling among you, are you not worldly? Are you not acting like mere humans? For when one says, 'I follow Paul,' and another, 'I follow Apollos,' are you not mere human beings?"* Rather than allowing themselves to be identified by the human leader they tracked with most, Paul insists that they identify the reality that they all, as one, have only one common leader—their Lord and Savior, Jesus Christ.

And again, where the first-century church was at risk of subdividing over differences in theology, Paul appeals for them to specifically not break fellowship over biases of interpretation. In Romans 14 (discussed in far greater detail in Chapters 6 and 14), he opens by encouraging them to *"Accept the one whose faith is weak, without quarreling over disputable matters."* In spite of differences in faith conviction, Paul expects these believers to do the work of remaining as one, even with others they feel, because of their personal conviction, are sinning. He identifies these believers not by their differences of interpretation but by their common faith in Jesus. (Even more radically, it is actually the theological diversity of the body of Christ, when we live in unity, that causes the church to grow into the image of Christ, as described in Ephesians 4 and 1 Corinthians 12!)

This is why denominations have never made sense to me, because while they're one part family, Scripture teaches that in Christ we're all one family. At another level, denominations function as communities of allegiance to the teachings of various human leaders, while Scripture insists we identify as one people under Jesus' common leadership. And where denominations have functioned like sects, distinguishing themselves through confessions of faith, Scripture appeals to all believers to do the work to actively unite as one voice of worship and service to Christ regardless of our biases and convictions. I can't help but ask, "Are denominations something that Jesus envisioned when he birthed his church?"

Missing Out?

When I read the Gospels, all I see Jesus envisioning is oneness for his people. In fact, I see him praying for this very outcome shortly before offering his life as a sacrifice for the sin of humanity. In John 17:20–21 Jesus prays, *"My prayer is not for [my disciples] alone. I pray also for those who will believe in me through their message, that all of them may be one, Father, just as you are in me and I am in you. May they also be in us so that the world may believe that you have sent me."* I don't see Jesus desiring for his people to be subcategorized as families, cliques, or sects, but as one people. And more importantly, I see a purpose in identifying as that one people: what Jesus specifically describes as the picture to be painted to the watching world.

In this day and age where the Christian church is known for being hypocritical, judgmental, and worthy of distrust, could this be a factor? Or, more importantly, could we as church leaders be missing out on a primary way that God intended to reveal himself to people? Over the years, I've been struck by how much church leaders will invest into evangelism. We attend evangelism conferences. We build evangelism departments and offer evangelistic programs. We beef up our weekend gatherings on special holidays to create evangelistic outreaches. In some cases, our churches operate with no higher value than the value of evangelism. But when we consider Jesus' one prayer in John 17, have we considered that perhaps we've neglected his primary evangelistic strategy, that instead of all these programs and initiatives, the way we'd compel the watching world to believe in the reality of the Jesus sent by God was through the oneness of his people? Have we appreciated in our heads Jesus' primary evangelistic strategy?

And, more importantly, have we allowed that value for kingdom oneness to sink into our hearts? Early on when our church relocated to be near the downtown core of the city of St. Catharines, I began to drive to work on a route that passed about a half dozen other local churches of various denominations. As I drove past them, I wondered what impact moving Southridge into that part of town would have on them, but, admittedly, I didn't care. As a younger leader, frankly, I had an arrogant sucks-to-be-you attitude, viewing other area churches more as competitors. Then one day I was chatting with a prominent local official, who out of the blue told me that my grandfather would be so proud of me. My mom's dad passed away when I was quite young but had been an Anglican minister up to that time. This local official, also involved in Anglican church leadership, told me how he was part of a small group of people, led by my grandfather, who planted the Anglican church in the part of town where Southridge had moved (one of the churches I drove by to and from work each day). And what was even cooler to him, was that the gatherings this small group held to pray and plan for this church plant happened in the very school that Southridge purchased in order to renovate and relocate to.

I was wrecked. To imagine my own grandfather saying the same prayers, leading the same kinds of meetings with the same creativity and optimism to shine Jesus' light to the world around that community, in the very same building I was now trying to do those very same things, had only resulted in me arrogantly thinking we'd probably put that church out of business by moving into that end of town. Is that what I wanted? Was that the way I wanted to contribute to the legacy of my grandfather's ministry leadership, by thinking that our church family, our community, and our version of Christianity was the only way God would effectively work? Since then, my arrogance has turned into prayers for the churches I drive by, knowing I've had a lot of work to do to embrace Jesus' vision of the oneness of his body and bride.

Practically Speaking

Over the years, I've appreciated the immensity of the challenge that fostering legitimate oneness among Christ followers can be. No wonder Jesus felt it was the one thing he had to specifically pray for! Even in the context of our local church, we've had to concede that not everyone will track with all of the nuances of Southridge, and that there's a certain ethos and culture that fits some people more than others. For some, this is a reason to further embrace the denominational dynamics where, like Baskin Robbins ice cream, there can be thirty-one different flavors of church for thirty-one different flavors of people. But that hasn't stopped us from aspiring towards—and practically functioning in growing ways as best we can—the direction of oneness that Jesus prayed for in John 17.

The first implication, maybe counterintuitively, was to not further subdivide by leaving our denomination, despite our differences and struggles with the idea of denominations. There was some sense that by identifying with a particular denomination we were sending the watching world a divided message, but we couldn't see how further dividing was the answer. So, we've sought to be active contributors to our denomination's activities. We have leaders on conference boards and provide resources to conference ministries, believing that we can do more together than we could alone. As well, we've acknowledged the value of a spiritual covering of accountability and have invited our denominational leadership into our processing and policy-development, most recently in our desire for a greater degree of LGBTQ+ inclusion as discussed in Chapter 14. We're not embarrassed to be part of our denomination and want to continue to grow in the kind of kingdom partnership we first inherited as a leadership.

At the same time, we're looking to functionally partner with anyone and everyone to advance Christ's cause. Our Anchor Causes are littered with strategic alliances—with government agencies, social services, and other ministries—to provide those on the margins with the most comprehensive support possible. This, interestingly, has also been recognized as an effective strategy by outside officials, who refer to this tag-team approach as a "hub-model" for social support. In recent years, we've gone so far as to apply for government funding in partnership with other agencies, even allowing them to take the lead, to paint a picture of active collaboration in an environment that is inherently fiercely competitive. United around common causes that are near to God's heart, we're aggressively deliberate to team up with anyone where "together everyone accomplishes more," regardless of their faith background. And we've begun to paint a compelling picture to the world around us of the unifying heart and Spirit of Jesus.

The other aspect we've sought to develop is our cross-denominational ministry network, specifically to demonstrate the oneness of the Body of Christ. Recently a movement has emerged out of southern Ontario called the "Jesus Collective," which seeks to galvanize and publicly identify as many people and churches around faith in Jesus as our centering point. We've aligned with ministries like the Global Leadership Network (which I also serve), who seek to develop leaders of all backgrounds for the common sake of advancing God's kingdom values in society. So, we're eager to band together with and learn from everyone. And in our local church ministry, we try to reach out to other area churches for both relationship and partnership, offering occasional ministry together and seeking to learn from each other's experiences in hopes that our surrounding society can see a church more united than divided today.

One Prayer

For me as a senior leader of a local church, I see this as more than just an aspirational future. I feel this as a personal obligation to Jesus as a follower of his. The more I've reflected on Jesus' one prayer in John 17, the more I've been struck by the fact that, with only a finite number of breaths left in his earthly body, he chose to only offer this one prayer. This one prayer for the oneness of his followers was the one thing he cared about enough to beg God for before giving up his life to death.

When I think about my own prayer life, that's convicting to me. While definitely not the world's best pray-er, I pray regularly, and in those prayers tend to ask Jesus for a lot. I can't imagine how many prayers I've begged Jesus to answer over the years, prayers for protection or provision, for guidance or grace, for strength or wisdom. And while I approach Jesus regularly with a revised laundry list of prayers I'd really love for him to answer, he only prayed for one thing and, here's the point: I can be part of the answer to it. Instead of focusing on all the prayers I want Jesus to answer of mine, have I absorbed the significance of the opportunity and obligation I have as one of his children to contribute my life to being part of the answer to his one prayer for oneness?

I'm not much of a bucket-list guy, but in the course of my lifetime I would love to be used by God to actively contribute to the merging of at least one set of Christian denominations. I would love to think that I could be used by God to reverse the picture the watching world sees today of forty-three-thousand-plus subdivisions of the Christian church, to instead see all of Jesus' followers be one in a way that the world could know the reality of the Jesus whom God sent. And I'd love to see that happen, not just for its evangelistic impact (although that certainly matters a lot to God!), but I'd like to contribute to something like that at a personal level, because at the end of my life I want to be able to say that I've given the best of my life to help answer Jesus' one prayer instead of spending the majority of my life only expecting him to answer all of mine.

What could happen if all of us committed to being the answer to the one prayer of the One who answers all of ours?

18

Leadership Development

ONE OF THE GREATEST contributors to my trajectory into vocational church ministry was the impact I experienced while attending a leadership conference. I can still remember the seat I was sitting in when I was awakened to the potential of the local church to transform societies. And I can still recall the palpable feeling in my spirit as I discovered the reality of the spiritual gift of leadership—not just teaching, shepherding, or other classically "pastoral" gifts—and the importance of leveraging it in expanding God's kingdom. I can still feel the conviction to give the very best of the rest of my life to what matters most in the world, God's Plan A, his church. That leadership conference I attended in August 1997, shortly before being invited by our board into a preaching and teaching role on our church staff, literally changed my life.

Since then, I've made a point of attending that leadership conference every single year, and encouraging as many as possible to join me, eager for an event like that to change their lives in similar ways to mine. And I've seen over the years, like the spiritual high of a week at summer camp for a kid, countless consistent stories of how, when people made space for God in extended, uninterrupted ways that such conferences provide, God changed their life dramatically. For the past fifteen years or so, Southridge has actually hosted a satellite site of this leadership conference, in hopes of sharing its impact with leaders all across the Niagara Region. Since those first trajectory-shaping days in 1997, there's always been a "conference junkie" in me.

Full, But Empty

About fifteen years ago, though, I experienced something surprising coming out of one of those conferences. It certainly wasn't because the conference itself was weak. To the contrary, it was one of the most impactful and highest-rated of its kind. That's what made the sensation so weird, because I returned home from the conference once again so filled in my spirit, yet at the same time sensed a void and a growing need that this large-group event wasn't meeting. The really interesting part was when I started debriefing the experience with other leaders who had attended the event and a number of them shared the same sentiment, that while full in their spirits, there was still an emptiness in their leadership development that this world-class event didn't fill.

Upon reflection, I realized that while the conference provided high-level inspiration, what I longed for even more was help with *my-level implementation*. Having attended this conference (and others like it) now for about a decade, I was tracking with the vision and heart it stimulated. And while valuable, if not essential to my leadership, what was increasingly emerging was the need for help in actualizing this vision in our local context. I needed voices who could speak into the granular, concrete challenges of local church leadership in my context in real-time, on-the-ground ways. The impact of the conference was excellent, but its high-level thinking felt distant compared to the up-close-and-personal ministry leadership support I was increasingly longing for.

The best I could summarize things at that time was in two ways. First, I felt I needed some colleagues who were in a similar stage of leadership and church development as me, in order to share our experiences and help one another navigate the complexities of local church work. I was reminded of the strength of friendship described in Proverbs 27:17, *"As iron sharpens iron, so one person sharpens another."* I longed for that kind of kingdom collegiality. As well, to prevent this cluster of like-seasoned church leaders from behaving as the blind-leading-the-blind, I also felt I needed a "coach" of sorts, a leader who was beyond where I was in their leadership and church development and having journeyed through the stages I was currently navigating, could speak experientially into my life and leadership. In a similar dynamic as the apostle Paul created, when he inspired people to *"Follow my example, as I follow the example of Christ."* I imagined this leader sharing insights I didn't even know to ask because of what they'd learned that I hadn't yet realized they could share with me.

As I shared these longings with other leaders, it felt like I wasn't alone. In spite of high-level inspiration, the our-level implementation of actualizing vision in our specific ministry contexts was by far our most pressing leadership challenge. The problem was: where could you go to find these like-minded, like-seasoned ministry-specific leaders who shared in the real-time challenges you were facing? And even more challenging: where could you find these coach-types who could share their on-the-ground experiences with you in ongoing, up-close-and-personal kinds of ways? There seemed to be no club you could join or event you could attend to meet those aching needs.

Old Testament Innovation?

As I continued to reflect on this challenge, I wondered whether this dynamic was something that needed to be built instead of bought. I was struck by the advice of Moses' father-in-law recorded in Exodus chapter 18, which is a commonly known passage for pastors because it forms the basis of how many of our local churches implement a mutual-member-ministry system and small group structure for pastoral care. In order for Moses to adequately address all the needs of the Israelites, and to do so in a sustainable way, Jethro encourages him to create an organizational structure of care for his people. In Exodus 18:21–22 it says, *"Appoint [suitable leaders] as officials over thousands, hundreds, fifties and tens. Have them serve as judges for the people at all times, but have them bring every difficult case to you; the simple cases they can decide themselves. That will make your load lighter, because they will share it with you."* Through this system of care, not through Moses providing all the care himself, the peoples' needs would be satisfied, and Moses' leadership would be more sustainable.

This captured the heart of what I felt I needed to support my development as a local church leader. While inspiring, I didn't necessarily need a Moses—in fact, often times it felt that, while a top-level senior church leader had amazing things to say, the scale at which they led wasn't relevant to my context, and the needs they faced were not directly applicable to the challenges we were facing in our local church. (Maybe you feel some of those dynamics even as you read this book!) In a sense, they were navigating the "most difficult cases" while I was still struggling with what, to them, would have been the "simple cases they can decide for themselves." To help me get unstuck in some critical ways, I actually didn't need the highest-level leader; I only needed the *next-level* leader who could specifically speak to my stage of development.

So, I started to imagine what it would look like to create an Exodus 18-style system of support specific to church leaders. What would it look like if a cluster of leaders of a similar stage in their leadership and church development convened together on a regular basis? And what if that convening was led by a more seasoned leader who had navigated their particular stage and challenges themselves before and could speak intelligently to the issues they were facing? And then, what would happen if each of these mentored leaders, in turn, created mentoring clusters of their own and invested in a cluster of local church leaders who were similarly stuck at stages they'd effectively navigated, to whom they could share their wisdom and experience to develop as well? What if the leadership development load was shared among many church leaders instead of relying on a few key celebrity church leaders to provide it for everyone? And what if these clusters could address more real-time issues in up-close-and-personal ways more constantly instead of waiting for the next silver-bullet insight at the next conference you attended?

My first ask was to a pastor in the Greater Toronto Area of Ontario, Canada who was leading a multi-site church far more complex than ours. At the time we were only contemplating making the shift to multi-site, but I knew if we were headed in that direction, this leader would be a terrific guide. So, I cold-called Tim Day, at the time senior pastor of The Meeting House, and shared these ideas with him. He responded politely, "Thanks. I'll pray about it," which I took to mean that he was not interested. (Isn't that the polite response pastors are trained to give to every request?!) But to my surprise, following up a couple weeks later I learned that Tim sensed God was in this and was eager to experiment with the idea. From there, we invited about a half-dozen other regional pastors into this mentoring cohort. What was most surprising to me, though, was that most of these already-busy church leaders didn't track with the idea at first until they were told that, as part of the deal, they would be invited to take responsibility to launch a mentoring cohort in their constituency as well. It was the take-*and*-give of this vision that captivated their imagination to participate.

The Model

This launched a fledgling pastoral support system that we called the Leaders' Village. We organized the layers of cohorts roughly according to current church size, not because attendance matters or because all churches are intended to do is grow numerically in weekend attendance. (I think we've covered that by now!) We chose to organize this way because the common dynamics and challenges in local church life seemed to be defined more by size of community than any other feature: two-hundred-person churches feel and function like two-hundred-person churches, but twelve-hundred-person churches face very different challenges, though they are similar to other twelve-hundred-person churches. In our case, we formed our cohort with churches of approximately one to two thousand people, which Tim led as the leader of a six-thousand-person multi-site church. Then, in turn, each of us facilitated our own local clusters of area pastors leading churches between two to four hundred people in hopes of speaking into the challenges they faced.

Each cohort met three times a year, once in the fall, winter, and spring. We met mid-week to allow time for settling from, and preparation for, the weekends between them. We met from 10:00am–3:00pm, a full space, including lunch, that allowed some margin before and after to still attend to any pressing issues that day. And we all attended the summer leadership conference each August in order to feed our conversations with the common language and inspiration of the world-class leaders the event convened.

Our agenda was divided into two parts: before and after lunch. Before lunch was a "prescribed need" prepared by the mentor leader, where they could add practical value in a way they felt timely that we may not have even known we needed. Lunch time provided a personal go-round but remained limited to lunch so as to not devolve into a makeshift therapy session. (This, as an aside, seems to be a common challenge to local ministerials, that drift away from the pragmatic and delve too deeply into waters where church leaders are untrained to navigate.) Then the afternoon was a free-space for individually specific felt needs to be addressed, where leaders could popcorn their questions to the mentor leader and they, together with the peer leaders, could share experiences and insights in response. This two-edged rhythm allowed leaders to be both invested in by a more seasoned leader, and fellow colleagues, while at the same time knowing there was space for their real-time pressing issues to get directly addressed.

This degree of customized, up-close-and-personal leadership development was greatly appreciated at each level of the cohorts we created.

In addition to the formal sessions though, joining a cohort also included you in the informal accessibility to the mentor leader and your colleagues. The mentor leader was basically giving you permission to enter into their world or bring them into yours. If in between cohort meetings you had a delicate board meeting or difficult conversation with a staff or volunteer ministry leader, you could connect on the phone or meet up for lunch and talk through it with the mentor leader. In this one-on-one opportunity, leaders could know they wouldn't have to navigate their real-time pressing leadership challenges alone. And the combination of formal sessions and informal accessibility became a rhythm that participating leaders celebrated. One extremely well-networked Ontario church leader in our cohort declared, "Leaders' Village is the single greatest leadership development investment in me in the past ten years!"

Reclaiming a Leaders' Village

After some years of initial expansion though, including the launch of a Leaders' Village cohort in Atlantic Canada, our movement floundered. What seemed integral to our effectiveness was the availability of a facilitator, someone who was freed up to coordinate the logistics of the cohort meetings. When we first launched, a staff member of a national para-church ministry was available to support this, but when their role was reduced, we lost that horsepower and the movement didn't continue to run by itself. This identified a more philosophical challenge, because if participating leaders were going to pay to free up another facilitator, suddenly the dynamics and expectations could feel transactional and not relational. But in absence of a financially supported freed-up facilitator role, busy church leaders couldn't consistently bear the burden of driving the leadership development movement themselves. So, while current cohorts still gather on occasion, adding critical value to those leaders, the movement itself has stalled.

Personally, I'm hoping that one of the impacts of this book is to reclaim the power of a Leaders' Village, one that networks local church leaders from across our country and around the world to navigate our local church leadership challenges together. As transformational as large-group, world-class leadership conferences can be, and have been in my own life and leadership, the up-close-and-personal, customized-to-my-context, ongoing real-time support that a Leaders' Village has provided has been game-changing. Now, I can glean wisdom and access support all 365 days of the year as opposed to the one or two where I'm attending a conference. And now, I'm not only inspired at high levels, but the daily challenges of personnel issues, ministry strategy, and change management are guided in community with my close church leader colleagues and our coach. We all agree that it takes a village to raise a family, but there doesn't seem to be a readily accessible, locally connectable network of developing leaders who, together, can help raise the spiritual parents of faith families around the world.

Like anything God does in powerful ways though, as is the point throughout this entire book, a movement like this requires devotion, not consumerism. The personal ownership of leaders for not only their own leadership development—but those of their peers, as well as those they would, in turn, invest in and mentor—is fundamentally not something that can be purchased. In conversations with leaders and leadership ministries over the years though, the idea of an Exodus 18-type support structure for pastors quickly devolves into how it could be monetized. But this degree of intensive and ongoing personal investment into, and as, leaders isn't something that can blossom, let alone sustain, when done transactionally. Even when we've applied the values and system of Leaders' Village to more niche-specific leaders, uniting children's ministry leaders or worship pastors, the effectiveness solely depends on the degree of ownership and devotion of the participating leaders. A movement of this nature is fundamentally built instead of bought.

Would you benefit from this kind of leadership development in your life? More importantly, could you *devote* yourself to an Exodus 18-style leadership support system, in order to benefit from it while benefitting others? As church leaders, we often recognize that life change happens best in relationship. But if leadership development is really only a specific kind of life change in a specific kind of person, then shouldn't leadership development happen most effectively in the crucible of ongoing, up-close-and-personal, real-time customized networks and relationships of like-minded and like-seasoned leaders?

We know it takes a village to raise a family. Could you use a village that specifically exists to help raise the spiritual parents of families of God?

Invitation

The Leaders' Village

Invitation

The Leaders' Village

IN THE SEASON WHERE I was processing entering into vocational ministry, my Dad wasn't thrilled with the idea. Growing up, my Mom (as described in Chapter 17, the daughter of an Anglican minister) was the one who regularly dragged my brother, sister, and me to church and encouraged a faith dynamic in our family. While my Dad was "busy" with other things, especially on Sundays, working our family's hobby vineyard. He also seemed evasive when it came to spiritual matters. So, he expressed his displeasure with the idea of me starting to work at our church. Feeling the importance, as a developing young man, of having their father's approval, I asked him, point blank, why he disapproved. At that moment, I finally found myself in a significant spiritual conversation with my Dad, as I had the chance to ask him, "Why are you not into faith and church?"

I will never, ever forget his reply. He told me a story of his day at work, that very day. My father was an elementary school administrator. He worked at a school in the Niagara Region located in kind of a "Bible-belt-ish" neighborhood. While it was a public school, it was the kind of school where Christian parents would inquire as to the spiritual status of their children's teachers at the beginning of each year, hoping their kids would have "good Christian influences." My Dad never knew how to answer that question, especially when it was asked directly of him. The best response he could give was, "Ask me in June."

In the season of our conversation though, the teachers at their school board were in a labor dispute with the provincial government. As an administrator, my Dad's responsibility was to mitigate the labor dispute at his local school, so he spent his days brokering the teachers' picket line while they were on strike. On this particular day though, the day I finally got into a conversation on personal spiritual matters with my own father, he explained to me that a number of the school parents (the same Christian parents who, every fall, insisted that their children be taught by good, Christian influences) were driving by and throwing tomatoes at the striking teachers.

I'll say it again: "Christian" parents were spending their day driving by a picket line of striking teachers to throw tomatoes at them in disdain. This, my Dad told me, was why he wasn't into the whole church thing. This was the reason he was reluctant to be enthusiastic as one of his kids considered vocational ministry by working at their local church. (Little did my Dad know at the time, but my brother would also become a pastor for almost two decades, and my sister would become a missionary who ran a Bible school in Japan! It's funny how God works.) At the time, in this significant conversation with my Dad, nothing was funny about what he shared. After telling me the story of the tomato-throwing "Christian" parents, he looked at me and asked, "Why would I want anything to do with that?"

I'll never forget the pained look on my Dad's face as we chatted at our kitchen table that day. And I'll never forget the blindingly clear sense I had walking out of my parents' kitchen. I had no response but to whole-heartedly agree with my Dad, conceding that to most people, the Christian church was experienced in a way best captured by Gandhi when he said, "I like your Christ. I do not like your Christians. Your Christians are so unlike your Christ." And while I'm not a defining-moments type of guy, I could sense palpably that I had one of two choices to make: either I could completely agree with my Dad and give up on the church as a result, knowing a generation later I'd be where my Dad was when it came to faith and church. Or I could completely agree with my Dad, but instead give the best of the rest of my one and only life to trying to fix that problem, hoping that a generation later my Dad would be closer to where I was.

The Calling of a Way-Finder

That, captured in a single story, and even a single question, has represented the bullseye of my life's calling for the past quarter century. All I've sought to get out of bed to do is to help make the Christian church make sense of Jesus to the watching world, so that people like my Dad could see who Jesus is through the picture painted by his people, and would run to God instead of away from him. In both our local context at Southridge, and through sharing God's innovative work with other leaders across Canada and around the world, all I want to do is help make Christ make sense to people through making his church make sense to people. As the bride and body of Christ, I understand the Christian church to be intended by God to be the manifestation of the life, love, and essence of Jesus, by the Spirit, to the world today, so I've sought to put my shoulder to the plow and help it become that to a greater degree. I want nothing more than for the Christian church to become—and be known for—the incarnational love of a Jesus who came to earth to be the incarnation of love to us.

With that goal in mind, together with the friends I've been able to serve with, our ministry has been quite simple: evaluating ways the church (or at least our local church) doesn't make sense of who Jesus is, and trying to fix them. As I referenced in Chapter 15, our strategy for changing a local church culture has been summarized as the "bottleneck approach," where we consider the greatest bottleneck to people seeing Jesus more clearly, completely, and continuously among us and then work to repair that aspect of our church's life. Once that bottleneck has been alleviated, we become aware of a new bottleneck that we hadn't seen before and embark on a new phase of the same work: making Christ through the church make sense to people.

As I reflect on this approach, it feels rather simplistic, but the more I interact with church leaders around the world, I find it's actually quite rare. A friend of mine who serves as a spiritual director in the world of spiritual formation once referred to me as a "kingdom warrior" like few others, saying that my tendency was to, "See where the fire was burning the hottest and run *towards* it instead of away from it." I'd never viewed my life or perspective that way but reflecting on that comment I would say there's a certain spirit that's required to take a bottleneck approach to cultural and systemic change that is not necessarily common to everyone. Yet as I connect with a growing collection of like-minded, like-hearted leaders around the world, there does seem to be a rare kind of kindred spirit that is emerging as a growing community of Way-Finders emerges. I'm far from the only leader whose passion is to make Christ through the church make sense.

What Makes a Way-Finder?

From my experience, there are at least four attributes to someone on the journey of *Finding Our Way*. The first is a bedrock conviction that the

Christian church is God's Plan A for redeeming and restoring the world, and that he has no Plan B. With that clarity comes a confidence that is willing to go all-in on the one entity on planet earth that is most invincible and indestructible. No matter how impotent or ineffective a local church may seem at any point in time, a leader can always rest in Jesus' promise to Peter when he said in Matthew 16:18, *"On this rock I will build my church, and the gates of Hell will not overcome it."* And a leader can know they're giving their life to the one thing that matters most to God in the world.

At the same time, a Way-Finder leader knows this isn't an easy road. In fact, especially when you consider the bottleneck approach as a culture-changing strategy, local church leadership in pursuit of greater Christlikeness can be a messy endeavor. But there's a tolerance to the challenge of it all that energizes this species of leader. They seem to actually embrace the mess. For me, a near life verse (and a core principle of our local church's leadership) is described in Proverbs 14:4 (NLT), *"An empty stable stays clean, but no income comes from an empty stable."* All of us have a choice of what will define our lives. We can pursue "cleanness"—orderliness, predictability, stability, and security—but that comes with a cost: lack of income. To pursue a life of "income" (not material wealth, but substantive return on God's kingdom investment) will necessarily generate a certain "messiness" within the stable of your life. A life of kingdom impact presumes and embraces a certain degree of messiness: complexity, challenge, and heartbreak. It's integral to living out and leading others in the legacy of Jesus. Way-Finders embrace the mess of leadership.

Along these lines, this type of leader knows they can't do it alone. In fact, the more they know about God and faith, the more they learn how much they don't know. This humble posture reaches out for help and can learn from anyone, even those they disagree with. And they're eager to partner, form networks, build alliances, and create cohorts because in their core they believe we're better together than alone. To them, the wisdom of Ecclesiastes 4 emanates from deep within: *"Two are better than one, because they have a good return for their labour. . . . A cord of three strands is not quickly broken."* These leaders know that to go fast you can go alone but to go far you need to go together.

More than anything though, what drives a Way-Finding leader ultimately has nothing to do with them. They insist on investing their lives for the sake of the integrity of God's name. This attribute, in fact, is what God meant when, in 1 Samuel 13:14, he referred to David as, *"A man after God's own heart.*" (Although this heart is far from limited to males!) In fact, while the story of David and Goliath is so often preached to inspire the courage to face the greatest challenges in our lives, the underlying tension of that narrative is that God's name was being defamed, by Goliath, and not one Israelite, not even King Saul, was willing to do anything about it. When David showed up though, he couldn't understand why no one was doing anything, offered himself and completely trusted that God would fight for him so that *"the whole world will know that there is a God in Israel."* The story of David and Goliath isn't ultimately a story of courage, although it certainly takes courage to face giant challenges. It's a story of the confidence and commitment of a leader after God's own heart to risk their whole life to fight for the integrity of God's reputation. That's what drives a Way-Finding leader.

It Takes A Village!

For the past quarter century, that's what's driven me and a growing number of friends and teammates in the Niagara Region of Ontario, Canada. And over the years we've learned that we're far from alone. There are seminary grads and stay-at-home parents, volunteers, and vocational ministers, whose hearts want to see the reputation of Jesus shine in their communities and around the world. They want to walk arm-in-arm with others to see that happen, learning from each other to actualize God's mission for the church, in order to realize his restorative vision for humanity. They're more than okay with the messiness and complexity of this journey, because they've given their lives to caring about the one entity on planet Earth Jesus cares about most: his body and bride.

If you're one of those people, I hope this book has been a helpful encouragement, not to direct you to where the church *should* grow, but to share some real-life thinking and practice of *how* it can grow in critical ways. More than that though, I hope this book can serve as a launch pad for greater networking and collaborating, yielding greater creativity and innovation, so that together we can see the church of Jesus Christ shine like never before, and so people around us can celebrate the integrity, welcome and inclusion, and credibility of Jesus, exuded through his people that they would be inspired to run to God and not from him. Because it takes a village to raise a family, those involved in parenting spiritual families need the strength and support of villages most of all. You can keep this journey going in your life and church by joining with us at leadersvillage.ca. We're eager to grow this movement of Way-Finding leaders committed to the practicalities of building comprehensive first-century churches in the twenty-first century that can shine the life and love of Jesus Christ to a world that desperately needs him.

For me, at first my commitment was to simply help my Dad see Jesus for who he really is. In fact, I joked with our church board when they first hired me that the day my Dad was in the baptism tank would be the day I could retire, thinking it would take a lifetime to make our church make enough sense of Jesus to a guy like my Dad. In reality, it only took four years. By far, the highlight of my ministry lifetime has been the opportunity to stand in the waters of baptism with my own father as he testified to embracing a "by grace through faith" personal relationship with Jesus. And the truly amazing part is that it wasn't a one-hit wonder. Since then, I've had the pleasure of watching my Dad and Mom grow together in their faith and lifestyles of full devotion, where today they're fixtures in our St. Catharines homeless shelter, revelling in the close friendships of their Life Group, and growing in their practice-based faith. What captivated him wasn't something he could consume but a way of life of love he could devote himself to.

Once I got the extraordinary opportunity to baptize my own father though, instead of retiring I realized that there were other dads and moms out there, and other people's kids, and other classmates and coworkers, friends and family members, teammates and neighbors for whom others would love nothing more than to see them grasp the reality of God's love for themselves. So, instead of packing it in after four years, I've continued on with my close colleagues in this forty-year vision, waging war on a tomato-throwing version of Christianity, seeking to comfort the afflicted while afflicting the comfortable, all with the hope of making Christ make more sense, by making his church make more sense, to more people. That's the adventure of a lifetime I hope you'll join us in.

For those of you carrying the burden of leading a local church, for those considering that type of calling, for those making the most of a ministry that's dear to your heart, and for those who want to see your church reach its full potential, even for the growing list of "Dones," people who've given up on the church because of the pain it can cause, I invite you into the adventure of *Finding Our Way*. I can't promise you it will be easy; in fact, I can guarantee it will be hard. And I can't promise you it will be quick. This era of restoration in the story of God's activity throughout human history exists in the already/not-yet dynamic we'll find ourselves in until Christ returns, that the Scriptures affirm will leave us groaning like a mother with birth pangs. But I can guarantee that it will be worth it, and that God will be with us. He'll strengthen us for the long haul, he'll guide us through the messiness, and he'll galvanize us together as he continues to advance his enduring purpose and shine his life and love to the world.

All of us have a choice. We can concede the Christian church doesn't make much sense to the watching world these days and walk away from it. Or, conceding the Christian church doesn't make much sense of Jesus, we can give the rest of the best of our lives to changing that. If you're inspired by that potential—and if you have enough faith to believe this is the one work God will pour out his Living Spirit to faithfully empower—then welcome to the adventure of *Finding Our Way*.